WHITEFISH CAN'T JUMP

& Other Tales of Gamefish on the Fly

E. DONNALL THOMAS JR.

RAGGED MOUNTAIN PRESS

CAMDEN, MAINE

TO LORI

Portions of *Whitefish Can't Jump* have appeared, in other forms, in *Gray's Sporting Journal, Game Journal, Flyfishing,* and *Alaska.*

Published by Ragged Mountain Press
10 9 8 7 6 5 4 3 2
Copyright © 1994 Ragged Mountain Press, an imprint of TAB Books. TAB Books is a division of McGraw-Hill, Inc.
All rights reserved. The publisher takes no responsibility for the use of any of the materials or methods described in this book, nor for the products thereof. The name "Ragged Mountain Press" and the Ragged Mountain Press logo are trademarks of McGraw-Hill, Inc. Printed in the United States of America.

Library of Congress Cataloging-in-Publication Data
Thomas, E. Donnall.
Whitefish can't jump, and other tales of gamefish on the fly / E. Donnall Thomas Jr.
p. cm
ISBN 0-07-064248-6
1. Fly Fishing. 2. Fly Fishing--Northwest, Pacific. I. Titles.
SH456.T49 1994
799.1'75--dc20   94-13837
CIP

Questions regarding the content of this book should be addressed to:
Ragged Mountain Press
P.O. Box 220
Camden, ME 04843

Questions regarding the ordering of this book should be addressed to:
TAB Books
A Division of McGraw-Hill, Inc.
Blue Ridge Summit, PA 17294
1-800-233-1128

A portion of the profits from the sale of each Ragged Mountain Press book is donated to an environmental cause.

Whitefish Can't Jump is printed on 60-pound Renew Opaque Vellum, an acid-free paper that contains 50 percent recycled waste paper (preconsumer) and 10 percent postconsumer waste paper.

Printed by R. R. Donnelley, Harrisonburg, Virginia
Design by Ann Aspell
Illustrations by Richard Harrington
Production and page layout by Molly Mulhern
Edited by James R. Babb

CONTENTS

FOREWORD

BY JOHN BARSNESS

O F ALL THE OUTDOOR QUESTS, fly-fishing has created perhaps the largest body of writing. At their worst, these narratives contain many strange conceits: the wild world as a stage for pomposity, the main actor an angler who, oddly, sees nothing wrong with impaling fish on sharp hooks and dragging them out of the water but would never, ever commit the "crime" of actually killing and eating one. At their best, fly-fishing books celebrate the world, in ways as fundamental as broiling a salmon fillet and as complex as all the rivers that lead to the sea.

Happily, *Whitefish Can't Jump & Other Tales of Gamefish on the Fly* is one of the latter. E. Donnall Thomas brings a number of irreplaceable gifts and skills to his book. Perhaps paramount is his skill with the English language. He likes writing, and over the years I've been his friend, fellow angler, and occasional editor, he's developed a style that, while spare and straightforward, never cheats you of the feel and look of the places he's been. And he's been many wet places, from the Bahamas to Siberia, and lived in other parts of the angler's heaven, such as Alaska and Montana. He travels not just with the poet's eye but with the scientist's mind, and just enough detached humor to let us know he cannot take himself too seriously. Enough that catching a fish often seems something of a surprise, as it should when it really happens.

There are hundreds of good fly-fishing books out there, some limited to how-to-do-it, others limited by river or region or species, or perhaps even the author. This one is not. It brings it all together—the fish, the places, and the people that can make something as simple as catching a wild fish not just a diversion, but a celebration of a way of life.

PREFACE

I AM FORTY-FIVE YEARS OLD, too young to be a curmudgeon, one of those insufferable old characters who hang around at boat launches and fly shops ruining everyone's day by pointing out how much better things used to be. But sometimes I feel that way about fly-fishing, an endeavor that has undergone a virtual renaissance within my lifetime. A space alien arriving on the Big Hole during the middle of the salmon fly hatch might conclude that the same sport an earlier writer had trouble distinguishing from religion is really about entomology, fashionable outdoor wear, and power, all of which is wrong. Fly-fishing is above all else about fish and the places they are found, and the celebration of this is why I wrote this book.

Knowledgeable readers will soon notice that this is not a comprehensive examination of North American gamefish. I neglected some important species such as Atlantic salmon and shad because I have never fished for them. I have met others, including smallmouths, walleyes, and pickerel, without forming the sort of intense personal impression that drives this text, and rather than risk embarrassment by pretending otherwise, I decided not to write about them either. In no case do these omissions imply a lack of respect.

The book is weighted heavily toward the gamefish of the Rocky Mountains and the Pacific Northwest. This could perplex some observers, who might wonder, for example, if any book needs to devote an entire chapter to *each* of the five Pacific salmon species. In defense of this regional bias, I can only say that I have written about what I know and care about. I would also point out that Alaska and Montana, where I have lived most of my adult life, are good places to call home if catching fish and writing about the process rank high on one's list of priorities.

Finally, if you must have a book written by an expert intent on telling how, retreat now before it is too late. This book is written by an enthusiast intent upon asking why, which is another matter entirely. The essential question of the last decade's writings on the subject— *Which fly?*—concerns me scarcely at all. I have sought instead to come to terms with the fish themselves and the places where I encountered them. These are the poles of the sport toward which my own internal compass has pointed all these years. If I have done my job, readers of these nineteen stories will come to understand why.

ACKNOWLEDGMENTS

THE AUTHOR WISHES to express his appreciation to John Barsness, for assuming the mantle of leading outdoor literary luminary; to Nick Lyons, for some marvelous unsolicited advice, some of which was followed and some of which was not; to Kate Myers of the University of Washington School of Fisheries, for helping unravel the taxonomy of the North Pacific salmonids; and to Jim Babb, for bringing just the right mixture of wit and enthusiasm to bear upon this project.

Some of the pieces in this book have appeared in print previously. One segment of "Bonefish Fools" appeared in *Gray's Sporting Journal.* Parts of "Humpies from Hell" appeared in *Flyfishing* and *Gray's Sporting Journal.* In somewhat different form, "The Prince of Autumn" appeared in *Alaska,* and "Gifts from the Sea" in *Game Journal.* I appreciate the opportunity to rework the material for inclusion in this volume.

ONE

BONEFISH FOOLS

Bonefish: *Albula vulpes*

THE KOREAN WRECK—*Te Kaibukenakawa* in Gilbertese—perches uneasily on the reef that forms the leading windward edge of Christmas Island. I have heard several speculative versions of its arrival there, tales that involve broken rudder cables and typhoons and the usual litany of hazards faced by sailors at sea. Somehow I suspect that none of them are true, that someone merely pulled an Exxon *Valdez*, fell asleep at the helm, and had the bad luck to hit one of the scattered microchips of coral that pass for landfall in the middle of the vast Pacific. It is tempting to read all kinds of symbolism into the presence of that rusted hulk—silent warnings, perhaps, about the failure of modern technology afoot in places where it does not belong. No matter. I am here because of the ocean flat behind the reef, a longtime favorite on my personal bonefish itinerary. It has been a long, cold winter back home and it has been a long flight south from Honolulu, made longer by the deadly *sake* hangover that followed me home from the sushi bar the previous evening. Now, finally, it is time to go fishing.

There are easier places to catch bonefish than the flat behind the Korean Wreck. Coral snags are scattered everywhere, and the rise and fall of the surge over the reef makes it more difficult to see fish here than on the white sand flats inside the island's leeward lagoon. The bonefish run smaller out here. Sharks cruise constantly through the cuts that extend through the reef, and there is no terrain to mollify the angry, incessant wind that pours straight in from the Pacific. Despite all this, the Korean Wreck is still the first place I go when I get to Christmas Island, because I sense that this flat and its fish will never disappoint me. And sure enough, they do not.

The first bone's take is visual rather than tactile, and when I lift the rod gently and haul on the line with my left hand I am reminded that I need to find more excuses to fish with the Fin-Nor. In many ways, it is an impractical reel. The brass frame is just too big and muscular for freshwater fish, and even anadromous species seldom justify its line capacity. It is meant for salt water, and I equate its authoritative feel with bonefish and the places I travel to fish for them. I love its weight and its cool metal presence and the smell of oil it gives off, but the essence of the Fin-Nor is the sound it makes when something takes a lot of line from it in a hurry. It is a smooth sound somewhere between a buzz and a whine, a sound that suggests fine tolerances on the part of the reel and a nearly magical source of energy on the part of whatever is making the spool revolve so fast. That is the sound of bonefish.

You seldom notice the departure of your fly line when you hook a bonefish. You feel the soft tug of contact at the end of the leader, and then the reel sings and the smooth wet belly of the fly line simply disappears from your hand, leaving you nothing but backing. So here I stand with the rod held high to minimize the chance of the line fouling, while the white cylinder of Dacron evaporates from the reel spool like an ice cube in a glass of warm gin. Meanwhile, the fish just keeps going.

This is a true ocean flat, with hard-packed sand underfoot and the steady pulse of breakers rising and falling beyond the reef, toward which the fish now runs with my line hissing through the shallows behind it. My fingers begin to explore the knurled margins of the drag, for if my quarry reaches the edge of the reef and plunges over the side into the blue water, fish and fly line will both be history. And still the fish just keeps going.

Which should come as no surprise. Going is what bonefish do best. As a matter of fact, the bonefish's short, sweet list of talents reminds me of another game species born and bred to survive in flat, open places: the pronghorn antelope. Pronghorns can see and they can run and that is about it. Of course, if you are a bonefish or a prairie goat, that is about all you need to do.

By one of those amazing natural coincidences, the duration of a good-size bonefish's first wild run is usually just a hair less than the line capacity of a Fin-Nor #2. Although I have seen brass peeking through the last reserves of backing on several occasions, I don't remember ever being truly spooled by a bonefish. True to form, this one's momentum finally runs down right at the edge of the reef, and at the edge of my backing. There will be a few more surges, but most of the remaining fight is simply reeling in, and unless I get unlucky with one of those coral snags the contest is all but over. The strike and the first wild orgiastic rush justify all it took to get me here. The rest is denouement.

Of course when the line is finally reclaimed, it is always worth taking a good look at the fish on the business end. This one is a representative but by no means exceptional specimen in the five- to six-pound range. I kneel and cradle it gently at sea level. Submissive without appearing exhausted, the fish wears an expression of resignation, and for a moment it is hard not to wonder if the object of all this attention is really anything more than a glorified sucker. There are some remarkable qualities to note before the release, however, that should lay such cynical notions to rest. The unnaturally brilliant iridescence of the scales in the sunlight suggests mysterious optical properties, of which we shall hear more later. The ballistic outline is a remarkable study in grace and efficiency, like a prototype design from a jet propulsion laboratory. The fish feels taut and muscular as it rests in my hand. And finally there is the faint, sensual coating of slime that remains on my skin even after I launch the fish back into the sea. I know that it will cling there, and that my hands will smell like bonefish for the rest of the morning no matter how many times I reach into the salt water.

And now it is time to wade on through the wrack and swell of the lonely flat and look for another fish.

In forty-odd years of enthusiastic living it has been my pleasure to do all kinds of wild and crazy things, few of which have lived up to their advance billing. I recall only two experiences that were absolutely, positively everything they were cracked up to be. One is not customarily done outside, at least not during the middle of the winter. The other is the pursuit of bonefish.

No matter their qualities at the end of a fly rod, if bonefishing required midwinter trips to, say, central Kansas, it would be unlikely to garner much of a following. Fortunately, this isn't the case. The serious bonefish agenda is a travelogue of exotic tropical locations. And while the pursuit of bonefish does not have to take place during the winter, it usually does, because that is when we need to do it.

By the sort of perverse logic that so often rules the realm of outdoor sport, I solidified my own bonefish credentials while living in Alaska. That's right, Alaska. In the first place, the Alaska economy made trips to bonefish country affordable, and the only thing reliably standing between a bonefish fool and a bonefish flat is money. In the second place, one's true, yearning *need* for bonefish varies directly with the latitude of one's principal residence and inversely with its mean winter temperature. When I hadn't seen the sun for weeks and the thermometer seemed stuck on thirty below, life was reduced to a matter of go bonefishing or die.

I went bonefishing, and never regretted the decision. These deficit-financed excursions took Sheli and me to most of the world's prime bonefish destinations. We kept running into the same people, most of whom were older and better heeled than us. We were on a circuit of sorts, and were lucky enough to have lived on two of the circuit's major stops (Alaska and Montana), which suggested that my life had not been squandered after all. I mean, there were folks who regularly paid thousands of dollars a week to do what I usually did in my spare time. This realization always made the cold back home more tolerable, and when the checks started bouncing afterward I could always tell Sheli that, viewed in perspective, our life on the fishing circuit was really a bargain.

We became obsessed. We named our first-born son Nicholas Turneffe, after the barrier islands of Belize where he was conceived. Sheli became a specialist and would fish for nothing but bonefish even when we lived in the middle of the best trout and salmon fishing in the world. When I drifted off to sleep at night I saw bonefish on the backs of my eyelids, not the anatomical details of individual fish but the coalescing and dispersing arrangement of abstract shapes that schools assume against the mosaic sand and grass background of the flats. I still do that sometimes, even here on the prairie where the ocean is a world away. Those are always the nights when I have the most comfortable dreams.

It is worth wondering about the kind of fish that can do this to you.

It begins with the eyes and the hallucinogenic quality of tropical light filtered through polarized lenses. Bonefishing is above all else a visual sport. You can stand and cast blindly into muds and catch a lot of fish doing so, but I was never quite sure why anyone would want to.

Seeing bonefish is legendarily difficult. It is impossible to tell someone how to do it. Some people never learn the trick—or tricks, actually, for there are several.

Standard advice, when available, encourages the novice to look through the water rather than at it. It goes on to point out that you are not really looking for fish but for something else, usually described as their shadows. That's good enough advice as far as it goes, akin to trying to tell someone quickly how to shoot a shotgun or call a turkey or perform any one of those similar Zen exercises that keep cropping up in outdoor sport.

The fact is, seeing bonefish requires the angler to look for many different things, depending on a whole host of variables including water depth, sun conditions, and the inclination of the fish on that particular flat at that particular time. It goes back to that mysterious optical quality of bonefish scales in sunlight, a visual stealth technology for which there must be some military application. We should be thankful that none has been discovered. A Bahamian friend once told me of netting bonefish by the thousand as a child and selling their scales for export to Detroit, where they were used to make hood ornaments for Cadillacs or some such thing. God knows what would happen to bonefish if the Pentagon decided that they had to have them. The amazing fact remains that bonefish can disappear before your eyes in clear water six inches deep. I've seen them do it.

And so looking for bonefish acquires magical qualities of its own. Sometimes you must look for shadows and sometimes for wave forms on the water, and sometimes you must scan for tail tips above the surface. Concentrate too hard on any one of these cues and you will not see any of the others. Search for the olive-green torpedo shapes of feeding bones and you may overlook the wave of nervous water heading toward you across the flat a hundred yards away. Shield your eyes against the sun and look for those energy waves and you may miss the tip of a forked tail protruding from the surface practically underfoot. What you get is what you see, and what you see is what you look for. It's tempting to read all kinds of conclusions into this business. A morning on a bonefish flat can become an inquiry into the nature of illusion and reality and the very basis of knowledge itself if you want it to. Go ahead. I do it all the time.

Once you understand that you're not simply looking for things that look like fish, you'll be ready to learn the tricks. You will learn, for example, that when you're trying to stretch another hour of fishing onto the end of a long day and the light is low and flat, you won't be able to see bonefish at all unless they're tailing. So you'll look for tails, and on the good evenings you'll see them. In deeper water you'll learn the trick of looking for the distant glint of fish feeding well beneath the surface, a visual cue that doesn't look like fish at all, but like the abstract shimmer that flakes of mica produce when you agitate the sand from the bottom of a mountain trout stream on a sunny day.

Let's assume that you have somehow managed to see the fish. Next, you'll want to catch them, a logical enough response given the miles you traveled to get wherever you are and the anticipation generated by all that bonefish mystique. You will be forced to ask the sport's most tedious and persistent question—*Which fly?*—and to answer it you will expect yourself to know what bonefish eat. Given the modern style of fly-fishing literature, you will imagine being able to offer up the menu in Latin, right down to proper scientific names for genus and species. That's how it's done, after all.

My own nihilistic view is that bonefish, like certain of our favorite people, are either in the mood or they are not. When you see a school of fish tacking aggressively back and forth in the surge like pointers working out the scentline of a running pheasant, and when those olive-green forms appear and disappear as the fish turn to and fro in the sunlight searching for things to eat, you can toss damn near anything in front of them and expect a pickup. If it doesn't happen, the fault usually lies with the presentation rather than the fly, which can be anything from a Crazy Charlie to a Bitch Creek nymph. (Don't laugh; I've done it). On the other hand, when you see a solitary bone sulking around on a falling tide looking bored and alienated and fundamentally unhappy, the problem of the near inevitable refusal will almost certainly not be solved by thumbing farther through the fly book. My own solution? If the fish are in that kind of mood, move on down the line and find some happier bonefish.

All of this takes place on saltwater flats, certainly among the world's most fascinating ecosystems, and one in which any student of natural history should have a good time no matter what the mood of the bonefish. The flats teem with life, all intent on the natural imperative to eat without being eaten. Here it is easy to imagine the great solar oven that incubated life from the primordial soup, to recall the days of trilobites and fish that walked on their fins. I happen to get off on that sort of thing, which is why I spend my slack time on the flats poking around in the mud like a wide-eyed kid rather than examining the contents of bonefish stomachs and testing new fly patterns like a *real* outdoor writer.

While the classical bonefishing of art and literature has the fly-fisher in the bow of a skiff and the guide in the stern, you can have that business as far as I'm concerned. Give me wading flats any day. In the first place, I'm a do-it-yourself kind of guy, and while I recognize the necessity of bonefish guides when it comes to getting you where you need to go, I'd just as soon they went off and did something else once we've gotten there. That's why I always bring along an extra rod. Furthermore, I like getting my feet wet. I like being down there at sea level with the rays and the boxfish and the crunch of coral fragments beneath my shoes and the sting of unseen marine organisms against my bare calves. Take that away and you have conceded the heart of the experience. I never did understand why anyone would want to give all that up just so they could look like someone else's idea of what bonefishing is all about.

This regard for wading flats explains my enthusiasm for two bonefish destinations above all others: Andros and Christmas Island.

There are flats in Christmas Island's vast internal lagoon that are never fished by sane people because they require hours of walking and swimming to reach. Needless to say, those are some of my favorites. There is a spit out there in the middle of all that sand and sun where I can get out of a truck and fish my way downwind all day to another pickup spot in the evening. The trick is that you have to swim a series of bluewater channels on the way, at which times it is easy to feel a bit like bait yourself. It will not help to read Captain James Cook's original description of the island, at which time his crew was unable to reach shore by launch because the sharks kept tearing the oars apart. This may explain why the Gilbertese society is the only subsistence maritime culture I have encountered in which nobody seems to know how to swim. Remind me sometime to tell you about our one brief attempt—against local advice—to spearfish the reef near the Korean Wreck.

Andros is probably the only other bonefish destination that can begin to rival Christmas Island for the extent of its wading flats. And Andros offers two distinct advantages over its Pacific counterpart: Caribbean ambience and *big* bonefish.

Somewhere around the ten-pound mark, bonefish undergo a transformation. While smaller ones are fun, bones weighing in double digits demand respect. These are the bonefish you anticipate and remember. Do this long enough and you will get to the point where you would rather try for one big one than succeed with many smaller ones, just as you will with trout or whitetails or any other species capable of producing real trophies, no matter what that means. There is no place quite like Andros for big bonefish, and no place quite like Andros for enjoying their pursuit. After all, grilled snapper and the musical Caribbean version of the Queen's English can be as much a part of the bonefish mystique as the sound of a screaming reel.

According to the calendar it is February, and I am feeling like a true bonefish fool. As the sun rises behind us from the Tongue of the Ocean, the early morning light seems lost between the glassy water ahead and the diaphanous layer of haze hanging above it, destroying all sense of distance and horizon. The little cays rising in front of us like ghosts could be a hundred yards away or a hundred miles. A school of baitfish appears in front of the skiff's bow and for a moment it is impossible to determine whether they're in the water or the air. The sea runs by so easily beneath us that I can scarcely feel it pass, and only the steady throb of the outboard grounds the senses in reality.

Ahead lies Andros Island's Middle Bight and the promise of big bones. I saw the biggest bonefish of my life out here somewhere a few years back, and the memory of that encounter has remained vivid ever since. It was the first day of the trip and my eyes weren't sharp yet, and so I stood and watched the thing glide past, so certain it was too big to be anything but a lemon shark that I didn't get a cast off until it was too late. I still remember being fixed by that piercing yellow eye as the fish slipped away into deep water. It was the kind of look to which a fool will always return.

Carl runs the skiff up into one of the maze of creeks diverging from the bight and we come to a stop at last. The silence and the eerie loneliness of the place trigger a sense of déjà vu, and finally I realize that the water and the scrub on shore and the combination of natural beauty and desolation remind me of Alaska. We have talked to Carl about hitting a hard-bottomed wading flat, but he wants to fish here from the skiff and I don't feel like arguing. We organize ourselves up front and Carl begins to pole, and we ease our way up onto the flat at last to the rhythm of his daily mantra: "All right, boneheads. Where *are* ya?" Suddenly, a shape appears in front of the bow, suspended in the strange, fluid mixture of air and water and light. Sheli manages a good cast but the fish ignores her fly as if it were invisible.

Carl is a man of strong convictions, and it is his opinion that the refusal is the fault of the fly, which he regards as too small and too light. This happens to be a pattern of my own design and I would ordinarily not brook such criticism lightly. An argument can always be made for keeping one's guide happy, however, so I fumble through my fly book looking for something big and ugly enough to do just that. It is too nice a morning for disagreement, and besides, there's always the possibility that Carl is right.

"Look at all those fish!" Sheli suddenly demands.

"I can't look," I protest, midway through a knot intent upon confounding my suddenly middle-aged eyes.

"Can we wade here, Carl?" Sheli asks.

"No way," he replies. "Too soft."

"I don't care," she announces defiantly. "I'm outta here."

I run the knot home at last and look up to see her strap on her belly bag and bail over the side of the skiff like a Marine. Sheli has always disliked the claustrophobia of fishing from a boat and will go to any length to avoid it. To the background of Carl's laughter, she manages to ooze a slow twenty yards through the marl, but that is all she needs. Phalanxes of feeding bones are tacking back and forth toward us across the flow of the tide. We cast downwind together toward the first wave of approaching fish and then all is chaos.

Bones in this intent frame of mind seldom disappoint, and these do not. We each hook up on the first cast, and of course the fish cross lines immediately. Somehow we untangle the lines and land them both, to Carl's great amusement. More bonefish advance toward us. The skiff drifts on past Sheli, who is soon fast to another fish despite being bogged down to her axles in marl. I pause to take a few pictures of her fighting her fish, but the lure of all those bones soon proves too much to ignore.

The onslaught lasts long enough for each of us to land several fish and hook several more, and then the flat goes dead for reasons known only to the bonefish. Carl offers an inevitable I-told-you-so on the subject of bonefish flies as we pole back upwind and rescue Sheli from the muck. The sun has finally risen high enough to burn through the haze, returning the optics of the flat to normal and breaking some kind of spell in the process.

We drift along casually before the current, enjoying sandwiches while Sheli dangles her feet over the gunwale to wash away the last of the mud from her toes. The furious pace of fishing has left us in a nearly post-coital state of satiety; there seems to be no hurry about getting on with the morning, or anything else. I close my eyes, stretch catlike in the sun, and try to imagine our Montana home locked in the hard grip of winter, but the image just won't focus. This is reality; the blizzards and the darkness and the air that bites flesh have become the illusion.

These are the moments in which bonefish fools are born.

There is a certain pointlessness to the best of fishing. The quarry is often inedible, and even when it isn't we often take great pride in our refusal to eat it. (Actually, I *have* eaten bonefish, but it's better if you don't ask about the experience. Imagine a hairbrush laced with cat food.) The best of fishing often involves expensive trips to faraway places where it is often too hot or too cold and things are just waiting to go wrong, where rod tips break and insects bite and the agents of exotic illness lurk in the drinking water. In such respects the best of fishing comes to resemble the best of almost everything else. no effort, no gain.

As a confirmed bonefish fool, I will go through the routine all over again next winter. I will look at the savings account and ask myself if kids really *need* to go to college these days. I will think up clever lies to tell my partners at work, who have wondered for years why the distant members of my family die only in February and why I always sport a tan when I return from their funerals. I will plead with the editors of outdoor magazines and the management of fishing lodges, and will shamelessly hurl promises before them like chum.

Fools cannot afford the luxury of pride. All I ask in return for sacrificing mine is the opportunity to see bonefish swimming across the backs of my eyelids as I dream my way to sleep at night.

TWO

THE BEST AND THE BRIGHTEST

Rainbow Trout: *Oncorhynchus mykiss*

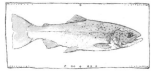

THE SUN PEEKED IN AND OUT of the summer cumulus clouds overhead as I sat on the abandoned irrigation pipe and studied the water gliding by below. It was late morning on my home water, a stream that shall remain nameless because it's a beautiful little creek, and watching it flow past is like watching my gorgeous adolescent daughter walk down the street: There are a whole lot of lowlifes out there who would like to ruin them both. The natural histories of undiscovered trout streams and pretty girls have a lot in common, and I reserve the right to feel protective toward both.

Ray and I had driven down to the lower reaches of the stream because the fish are generally bigger below town and because the ratio of browns to rainbows is higher. I wanted to catch a presentable brown for purely mercenary purposes: I needed a photograph of a brown with a particular fly in its mouth to accompany an article whose sale was going to cover the credit-card charge from my last trip back to Alaska. If I have learned anything about the business (for want of a better term) of outdoor writing it is that this sort of calculated approach to hunting and fishing is almost inevitably a mistake. Most of the time, you manage not to do whatever it was you set out to accomplish, and this failure winds up ruining an otherwise perfectly good day. In other words, I should have known better.

It was early June and a complex series of hatches had been coming off the water right at midday. Pale Morning Duns were the featured attraction, but fish had been rising to caddis as well. On creeks like this you never really know until you get there, so I chose to sit and wait from a vantage that afforded an excellent view of the water and a safe haven from the rattlers that were beginning to stir along the banks in the early summer sun.

At first there was no activity at all, which is just what I expected, but the lack of business down in the creek was anything but a problem. Sheli had moved out of the house recently and it was obvious she wasn't coming back. Her decision had left me to deal with the challenge of single parenthood as well as a certain unaccustomed measure of loneliness, and even with the arrival of the Pale Morning Duns it had not been an easy week. I kept telling myself that if catch-and-release worked for fish it ought to work for women as well, but this rationalization was starting to wear thin. I was ready for some hydrotherapy, the kind of emotionally neutral self-hypnosis that comes from watching a creek go by when there are no feeding fish to make me feel like a predator. I studied the dried turd sitting next to me on the irrigation pipe and tried to imagine the raccoon that had left it there, claws on rusted metal, balancing adroitly twenty feet above the water gurgling past in the night. Then a muskrat emerged from the water and began to feed in a patch of grass right underneath me. The light was too harsh to arouse my photographic instincts, so I just watched and let the sun warm my back and listened as the creek babbled its way downstream on the first leg of its long journey toward the Mississippi.

I heard rather than saw the first rise, and that almost always means that the responsible fish is a large one. I shifted involuntarily at the sound, and the muskrat spooked from the noise and hurled itself into the water; by the time all this flight-or-fight nonsense was over everything was hiding in bed with the covers over its head including the trout. I could see PMDs coming off the water now, looking like little flecks of gold dust ignoring the law of gravity and rising away from the center of the earth. The mayflies proved too tempting for the fish despite the muskrat's rude disturbance, and soon the run beneath the pipe was alive with surface-feeding activity. For better or worse, I could be a passive observer no longer.

I crawled across the pipe and dropped down to the bank. Irrigation and the previous evening's set-your-clock-by-it thunderstorm had added a touch of color to the water, but this was at most a minor aesthetic liability. An angry boil appeared out in the current where I had marked the best fish rising, and I dropped a no-hackle dun right on the money.

Nothing.

After the fish ignored several more perfect drifts it was clearly time to go back to the drawing board. Several smaller trout rose next to the bank and I sat down to watch them dine. The mayfly hatch was steady but not overwhelming in volume. Several duns drifted down through the run unmolested. Then a single #14 tan caddis fluttered across the water and disappeared at once into just the sort of slashing rise I had witnessed earlier. The caddis was the same color as the flank hair from the whitetail buck I had arrowed the previous November, hair that now resided mostly in my fly box. I replaced the no-hackle dun with a deer-hair caddis pattern and flicked it into the big trout's dining room, confident of the triumphant combination of the scientific method and the rational mind.

When the trout took the caddis, none of the bullshit mattered anymore. The fish was right there in the sunlight, as long as my forearm, pink and silver, jumping at the touch of the hook in that hysterical fashion unique to rainbows, not caring where their leaping takes them and acting as if air and not water is their natural element.

Hooking a red-hot twenty-inch rainbow on a 3-weight rod is like grabbing a charged wire fence by accident: It is clear that something out of the ordinary has happened, but for an instant it's not quite clear just what. While I stood and stared at the creek with a *What hath God wrought?* expression on my face, the fish stopped jumping and started running. After two quick, flashing circuits of its home pool, the trout headed downstream, and I was soon well into my backing and the fish was well below the irrigation pipe where all of this had started.

In small water like this, fish either break off on an obstruction or run out of places to go. After its final downstream surge the rainbow wound up panting in a languid little backwater, and there was nothing left to do but reel my way down to it. Utterly spent, it simply lay there with the deer-hair caddis looking like a freckle on its jaw. The trout's colors were just right: pink enough to appear vital but not so dark as to suggest the lassitude of recent spawning, splashed with a kaleidoscope of black markings. I flicked the dry fly from the corner of the fish's mouth and cased it back into the current, remembering with a sudden Protestant-work-ethic flash of angst what it was I had come for that day. Fortunately, something about the sight and the feel of a fish like that cleared the mind: What brown trout? What article? What credit card?

Hell, what ex-wife?

Thank God for rainbows.

I admit to some unease regarding the subject of this chapter.

In a sense, it's easy to write about grayling and pike and pink salmon. Most fly-fishers have never dealt with these species, and the few who care will be so tickled to see their secret pleasures mentioned in print that they'll let you get away with almost anything.

Rainbow trout are another matter. Everyone has a rainbow story, and a lot of them are as good as anything I have to offer. Presume to write about rainbows and you immediately find yourself in heady company. The rainbow trout is to outdoor writers what Hamlet is to actors or compulsory figures used to be to competitive ice skaters: an impossible standard that one must approach with a mixture of reverence and duress.

The urge to report something new can be overwhelming, however, so it may be appropriate to begin with the rainbow's biological classification, even though few of its characteristics would seem less subject to change. Guess again. While the revisionist scientific name *Oncorhynchus mykiss* appears in this book's table of contents, I would have preferred the previously traditional *Salmo gairdneri,* for no other reason than my own wistful sense of history. In fact, all North Pacific salmonids have recently been welcomed into the *Oncorhynchus* clan. The logical response from those more interested in catching them than analyzing their DNA may well be *So what?,* but this is one instance where the fuzzy edges of biology may be more interesting than they seem. Students of such matters and alert readers of this book will recognize *Oncorhynchus* as the genus of Pacific salmon. The specific name *mykiss* historically applied to the Russian version of the rainbow. The term derives from a Westernized version of the indigenous name for the fish encountered on the remote Kamchatka Peninsula by one Johann Walbaum as far back as 1792. In the 1980s, sophisticated genetic studies demonstrated that the New World steelhead and the Kamchatka trout were one and the same. Because of the historical precedence of the Old World term, our steelhead became *mykiss,* a reasonable gesture that at least emphasizes the pan-Pacific origins of this splendid fish. Soon the inland version of the rainbow was *mykiss* as well. I suppose it's nice to know that steelhead and rainbows are still the same thing even if both turn out to be Pacific salmon after all. Personally, I could have gone right on calling the rainbow by its nineteenth-century scientific name *irideus,* which I find both descriptive and lyrical, but then nobody asked my opinion.

The eventual inclusion of all the western trout in the genus *Oncorhynchus* is as an appropriate reminder of these fishes' recent evolutionary links to the sea, but it's still vaguely unsettling to those of us with a strong regard for fly-fishing tradition. Do we really want to acknowledge family ties between the fish described in this chapter's opening paragraphs and a decomposing pink salmon? One has to wonder what we would do without those rascal biologists who seem to delight in upsetting our sense of order. One can interpret this confusion as a measure of the natural world's complexity, the perfidy of scientists, or the hopeless romanticism of fly-fishers and those who write about fly-fishing. Take your pick.

All of this does help us amateur scientists to remember the rainbow's origins, however, something to keep in mind now that human enthusiasm has made the fish ubiquitous throughout the fresh waters of the world. For the rainbow did not evolve in spring creeks or farm ponds, but in the wild and unsettling North Pacific, a simple historical fact that does much to explain many obvious elements of the rainbow's character. I've listened to (and participated in) my share of pound-for-pound disputes about the identity of the world's greatest fighting fish, and I don't want to hear any more about it. It's the rainbow, stupid.

I've heard all the arguments to the contrary. One reason that advocates of Atlantic salmon and permit and whatnot feel as impassioned as they do about these exotics is that after doing what you have to do to catch one (time, money, pain in the ass), you had better believe you have done something incredible or you will begin thinking about what a fool you really are. After all, imagine how many *trout* you could have been catching instead. I am reminded of the nearly hysterical enthusiasm for sheep meat expressed by most sheep hunters. Sure it's good, but it's not that much better than moose or elk or caribou. Try telling that to a hunter sitting down to a meal of fire-blackened sheep ribs who has spent two weeks running up and down mountains after a ram.

All *mykiss* may have been created equal, but they certainly haven't survived generations of human meddling on equal terms. The clan now includes hatchery steelhead, whose purpose is little more than to occupy space, and the Donaldson trout, engineered to grow prodigiously and make people money. Such biological triumphs come at the cost of wildness, and even people who should know better sometimes lose sight of such distinctions. Those who have taken pure native rainbows from strains that haven't been messed with will have no problem comparing such fish favorably to anything the world has to offer on the end of a fly line.

It is the middle of August. We are floating a remote drainage in southwestern Alaska. The river has been turning and tumbling for thirty miles with no place to land a plane on floats or wheels, which is why you have never heard of it. To get here, we had to set down on a lake and carry our gear across several miles of brush and tundra before we started to float. Most people just aren't willing to do that kind of thing—and they don't, which is why I love this particular river so much.

We are bowhunting for caribou. We have not yet seen a decent bull, much less shot one, which is fine with me. The weather is uncharacteristically hot—if we had taken an animal I would be worried about the meat—and my attitude toward a perfectly good float trip might be hopelessly compromised.

There isn't any really tricky water here, and other than watching for unexpected sweepers there is little to do but let the current carry us along. It is a suntan, shirt-sleeve kind of day, and anyone who fails to appreciate how unusual this is cannot have spent much time in this country. Joe seems nearly asleep at the oars, for which I cannot blame him. In the bow, I have nothing to do but fish and swat bugs and glass the hills casually for game.

We are a bit too far inland for early silvers. A few dark pink salmon lie scattered along the bottom, but they're way too funky to be of any real interest. I am dead-drifting an Egg Snot Fly along the bottom. This pattern of my own invention looks like something left behind after an evening of lust on the spawning redds. Though a fly only in the loosest sense of the term, it is highly effective on most Alaska gamefish whenever there are spawning salmon about. Besides, the Egg Snot Fly doesn't take much technique to fish properly, which makes it well suited to a day like today when most of my attention is focused through my binoculars on the nearby sidehills.

I have been catching grayling at a steady if not spectacular rate. They are beautiful and large enough to be of interest, if not quite large enough to make me put my field glasses down and fish like I mean business. You don't hear much about using egg patterns to catch grayling and I don't know why, because they certainly work, as the bedraggled Egg Snot Fly on the end of my leader can attest. Still, they are only grayling, and except for the quick jolt of surprise at the strike and the moment of admiration before the release, there isn't much more to be said about them.

Then the line hesitates again and I raise the rod tip without thinking, but this time everything is different. The rod kicks back like a mule and suddenly all is chaos onboard the raft. I drop the binoculars and try to come to terms with the undisciplined tangle of line strewn about the bow. There are loops everywhere, wrapped around everything, and it doesn't seem possible to get them all out of the boat and running free, but suddenly the reel is screaming and I know that I've done just that.

Aroused from torpor by the excitement, Joe is flailing helpfully at the oars. "Silver?" he wonders aloud.

"I don't think so," I reply. The ratio of energy to weight seems a bit too high, or something like that. Then the fish is out of the water and up in the sunlight with its pink sides on display, and suddenly it becomes very important that we land it.

My attention is on the fish as we drift on around the next bend and so is Joe's, and so his sudden cry of alarm comes as something of a surprise. When he yells *"Jesus!"* at the top of his lungs, however, it's obvious that he intends something more than a sudden reaffirmation of his lapsed Irish Catholic faith. Then I take my eyes off the spot where the line has disappeared into the current next to the bank, and there is the bear.

I've spent enough time trying to get close to grizzlies to make too much out of simply seeing one, but this is a unique situation. We have come upon the bear without warning. The bear is obviously surprised and confused, and those are not desirable traits in grizzlies. The bear is swimming in the middle of the river and we are bearing down on it faster than any of the involved parties want. The bear seems to turn to the left bank and Joe pulls to the right, but then the bear turns and thrashes to the right as well, and even though none of us wants to be any closer than we already are, the possibility of a collision between boat and bear seems to be acquiring a life of its own.

The bear has finally gotten some bottom under its feet and is lunging about in the water as Joe flails at the oars with an equally inefficient ratio of noise level to results. The fly rod lies forgotten against the side of the raft as I try to locate the 12-gauge pump in case it comes to that. Then suddenly the bear, now clearly an honest nine-footer, is scrambling catlike along the gravel bar and spattering us with river water as he shakes and runs. Joe gives one last mighty pull on the inside oar and we spin past, awash in the giddy flush of survival.

Then the rod tip slaps me in the face and I realize that against all odds the fish is still on the end of the line. Joe pulls wildly on the oars, sending me to my knees as the raft pivots. Line is everywhere once again. I stumble helplessly as Joe rows, and then we're in the shallows next to the opposite bank. Somehow my legs gather beneath me and I'm out of the raft at last, playing the fish with some sense of control. After two more runs the rainbow is there in the quiet water at my feet with the Egg Snot Fly hanging from the angle of its mouth like an orange survey marker. It's hard to imagine that any fish could fill the hole in the day left by the craziness with the bear, but this one somehow does just that. Lying quietly at my feet, it looks to weigh five or six pounds and carries more perfect black spots on its side than you can imagine fitting on one rainbow, a unique local signature of the fish native to this area. Finally, there isn't much left to do but release it and watch it swim back into the current.

What caribou? I wonder silently as I organize the line and prepare for my shift at the oars. What mosquitoes? What ex-wife?

Hell, what nine-foot grizzly?

Yes, thank God for rainbows, the best and the brightest by whatever name we choose to call them.

THREE

BIG BROTHER

King Salmon: *Oncorhynchus tshawytscha*

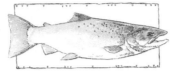

ALASKA'S RENOWNED KENAI RIVER heads high in the mountains of the same name, collects itself in the almost painfully blue waters of Kenai Lake, and puts the finishing touches on its rugged character as it sweeps on down through Skilak Lake and past its great glacier. For the next fifty miles it becomes the Far North's most popular sport fishery before finally emptying into Cook Inlet. In the process, the Kenai plays host to much of what is both wonderfully right and sadly wrong with the Alaskan outdoor experience.

There is much to admire about the Kenai along its short, brawny course. The river's upper reaches are home to a wealth of wildlife. I have hunted bear and moose and caribou and sheep in those mountains, and if there is more gorgeous alpine scenery anywhere I have yet to find it. On one afternoon canoe trip downstream from Skilak Lake during the peak of the spring migration I counted over sixty species of water birds. The Sterling Highway, which parallels the river for most of its course, is one of the few places in the world where you can hear wolves howl from a paved road.

There is much here for the fly-fisher to admire as well. The upper Kenai is one of the world's great underappreciated trophy rainbow fisheries. Come August the lower river fills with some of Alaska's largest silvers, and you can fish for them in near solitude until winter arrives one day and chases you from the water. And then there is the matter of the kings.

Kings occupy a unique position in the pentarchy of Pacific salmon by virtue of their size. The smallest kings are larger than all but the very largest silvers and dogs, and they dwarf most reds and pinks. To anglers who make no distinction between big fish and best fish there is really nothing more to say. The Kenai carries this business of size to unequaled and nearly unbelievable lengths. Unique genetic factors have made Kenai kings larger than those found anywhere else by a factor so substantial that one has to wonder at times if they are really the same fish as their relatives from other waters. (The biologists assure us that they are.) When I was growing up on Puget Sound, a forty-pound king was bragging size; a fifty-pounder a rare trophy. On the Kenai, those are just everyday fish. There, anything much under seventy won't earn you a second look, eighty-pounders are taken every year, and when the new world record was finally hauled from the lower river to tip the scales at just under the three-figure mark, no one who knew the Kenai was surprised. I could never confirm the persistent local rumor of the hundred-and-twenty-five-pound king that showed up one year in a Fish and Game netting sample, but I suspect that the rumor was true. There is just no place else on earth that produces salmon like these.

Which is a large part of the Kenai's problem. Something about exceptionally large gamefish makes people just have to have them, the way empires have to have colonies or Imelda Marcos has to have shoes. Large numbers of people who want anything from the outdoors badly enough have the potential to stress valuable resources. As the reputation of its salmon grew, guiding on the Kenai went from a cottage industry to Big Business in only a few years. By the time I finally left the area, there were hundreds of loosely regulated guides on the water there, most of whom could be found concentrated on a few limited miles of the lower river during the first two weeks of July. Needless to say, the mob scene is one reason why I left.

Guides and crowds were part of the problem, but they certainly weren't all of it. The river's kings return in two pulses: The first wave arrives in May and June and contains smaller fish, although the early run is certainly my favorite for reasons we shall explore later. The second run contains the big fish and arrives in early July. By this time the river's substantial return of red salmon is also beginning to work its way along the east side of the Cook Inlet, where set-net fishermen are ready to harvest them commercially. Unfortunately, there is no way to catch those lucrative reds without catching a significant number of kings as well, and gillnets were never meant for catch-and-release fishing.

When two powerful interests with substantial sums of money at stake vie for control of a wild resource, the results are seldom pretty, and the struggle over the late-run Kenai kings proved no exception. Things got so ugly so fast that it was sometimes difficult for people like me to remember why we cared in the first place about the fish fighting their way upstream through that opaque glacial water. But I do remember.

Do I ever.

It is early June. The ice and the low-country runoff are gone, but the glacial melt that feeds the river all summer has not yet started down the line in earnest, and the water is as low as it will be for months. For technical reasons that will soon become apparent, this is a prime consideration for anyone ambitious enough to try for a Kenai king with fly tackle. It is these low-water conditions coupled with the relative absence of crowds that explains my preference for the river's early run of somewhat smaller fish.

With the work day comfortably behind me at last, I pick my way downstream in the boat, following the familiar passage through the shallows below its moorage at my neighbor's house. Finally, I turn into the bank and drop the anchor. This is one of the few stretches of water in the river where it is feasible to fish for king salmon with a fly. For the next two weeks it will be my home whenever I'm not working or flying somewhere, and since the long arctic twilight allows fishing nearly round the clock at this time of year, I can already anticipate the same giddy ecstasy of sleep deprivation ordinarily found at adolescent slumber parties.

As the boat drifts gently with the current and snubs up against the anchor rope at last, I ready myself as if preparing for a space walk. There is no argument for neoprene waders quite so persuasive as a glacial river. The odd combination of fingerless woolen gloves and insect repellent completes my June king-fishing ensemble, and then I'm over the side and belly deep in the turbid green water.

Fly-fishing for king salmon always imposes special demands; in glacial rivers, it sometimes seems less an art than an act of penance. No anadromous fish loves the sweet slick of laminar flow at the bottom of the river quite like the king. If the fly is not down there it may as well not be in the water at all. And then there is the matter of visibility. Because Skilak Lake acts as a settling basin, the Kenai is less discouraging in this regard than are many glacial streams, but it is still difficult to imagine a fish being able to see a fly down there in all that murk and darkness.

These challenges explain my choice of tackle from one end to the other. The fly scarcely qualifies as such, consisting of a huge, sharp hook coated with lead wire, brilliant orange yarn, and a plume of equally brilliant orange marabou half the size of my hand. Before you turn up your nose, remember that its job is simply to get down deep and be seen once it's there. The leader is an eighteen-inch length of twenty-pound-test mono, because it must survive the beating it will take along the bottom—and there are no leader shyness problems in water as turbid as this. The line is a high-density sink-tip, since the casts will all be short and a shooting head concedes too much critical line control. The rod is a 9-foot for 10-weight, and in the hours to come I'll need every ounce of its muscle. And finally there is the reel, which comes right out of my saltwater equipment bag. This is one of the few situations in fresh water that truly justifies its tolerant drag and generous supply of backing. Should everything come together down there in the cold and gloom, a hefty king propelled by all that current can eat up every foot of it.

This is a unique hundred yards of river. A long, even slot here holds migrating kings, and a small feeder stream contributes a delicate taste of relatively clear water along the bank before it is lost to the main river's glacial surge. The fish will be playing peek-a-boo in and out of the junction between the two flavors of current, and the idea is to have the fly right there on the bottom where they can whack it when they do.

The fishing itself is an inelegant, nothing-but-the-basics affair. I slide over the side of the boat, take a measure of the current bearing down against me, and wade out as close to the line of demarcation as I can manage. To get the fly down where it needs to be, I must cast nearly dead upstream, and even then I can barely keep up with the current as it sweeps the line past. After three casts I have yet to feel the bottom. I pull in the fly (it looks like a drowned orange bird by now) and add ribbon lead to the leader. The brief tick of hook on rock at the end of the next cast tells me I'm fly-fishing for kings at last.

After a dozen more casts I am in my rhythm to stay: lift, haul, cast, mend, strip, lift. . . . If I were doing anything other than fishing this would feel uncomfortably like work. I go gently numb below the navel as the frigid water sweeps past toward the sea. A boat appears from downriver and I brace myself, but the guide is a friend who understands; he turns wide and we part company with a friendly wave. It does not always go so well.

The fact is, almost no one fishes for kings in the Kenai River with fly tackle. There are good reasons for this, of course. In the years I lived there, I never saw anyone else fly-fishing the Kenai for kings who was not a personal friend, which may simply illustrate the old aphorism about misery loving company. The fact is, anyone beating the Kenai's frigid water with a fly rod can expect to be taken for a lunatic.

Because kings reveal less of themselves in fresh water than any other salmon species, fishing for them requires above all else a measure of blind faith. During the course of every third or fourth drift the fly hesitates briefly against the bottom, and I strike as if it might be the real thing, adding syncopation to the monotonous rhythm of cast, drift, and mend. The light has acquired the eerie, directionless quality unique to summer nights in Alaska. A bald eagle flies up the river as another guide boat drifts by, and boat and raptor converge and pass by with no indication that they have even seen one another.

Cast, drift, mend. . . . After a solid hour of this the line hesitates one more time and I strike reflexively. This time the sensation in my hand is soft, heavy, nearly unbelievable. I strike again, this time so hard I almost lose my balance in the current, and then there's nothing but the feel of the fish disappearing downriver and the echo of my own primal scream.

No freshwater fish on this continent conveys quite the sensation of pure force on its first run as an ocean-bright king salmon. Any attempt to describe it becomes a cliché: They are like freight trains, lightning bolts, wild horses—you know. The hell with it. The fact is, despite being geared up for big game, I am now entirely at the mercy of this fish.

The battle is technically a no-brainer: Just crank the reel's drag down as far as it will go, keep the rod tip up, and hope. Either the first downstream run will exceed my line capacity or it won't. The bank is too rough and cluttered to allow pursuit. Out in the powerful green water the fish shakes its head and bulls its way forward, and there is nothing left for me to do but hang on.

A hundred yards below me the fish stops and sulks. I struggle back toward the bank where I can at least maneuver a little without having to battle the full force of the current. The trick to landing a heavy king on light tackle in a powerful river like the Kenai is to apply a nearly insane amount of pressure. Anything less and you'll wear out before the fish does. Remembering that it is almost impossible to break a twenty-pound-test leader with steady pressure from a graphite rod, I grind the butt into my abdomen and lean into the fish with everything I've got.

The fish yields, slowly at first, and then the line begins to tear back upstream. I pump and grind, but only the pressure of the current against the slack line's great lazy belly keeps any tension on the hook at all. Another boat appears and for a minute it seems intent on colliding with my line and my fish, but at the last minute the pilot recognizes my situation and veers toward the other side of the river, and all is clear. A quick wave is all I can spare to acknowledge this courtesy.

Still unseen, the fish draws abreast of my position and stops. Nothing moves for so long that I'm afraid the line has fouled—

although clean, scoured bottoms are among the few user-friendly features of glacial rivers, without which landing a king on fly tackle from shore would be almost impossible. The rod is bent nearly double and it occurs to me that I could be doing some kind of testimonial endorsement for its maker. Overhead the eagle returns, its plumage gone gray in the featureless twilight. Again the bird ignores the drama below as it glides back downriver toward the sea.

Finally I begin to regain some line in earnest. My rod hand can feel the fish itself now, rather than the abstract weight buffered by all that current. The off-set color of the sink-tip appears, then the butt of the leader, and then, like a child's Christmas present emerging from its last layer of wrapping paper, the fish itself is there in the shallows. At first there is only a wake in the water, but then I can see the incredible length of the shape beneath the surface, and then a tail and a dorsal fin, and finally I can take a proper measure of the quarry that fought out there with such determined anonymity for so long.

King, Chinook, spring, tyee . . . *Oncorhynchus tshawytscha* has more sobriquets than any other Pacific salmon—inevitable for a creature whose real last name contains eleven letters but only two vowels. Most of these names celebrate either the fish's size or its early return to fresh water after the rigors of the long northern winter, which earned it a special welcome from the appreciative natives of the North Pacific coast. I have always been partial to the colloquial term tyee, a beautiful, lyrical name derived from the Nootka word for big brother.

Certainly the fish now making its final surges of resistance against the line could be the big brother to almost anything ever found in fresh water. Although just another fish by the skewed standards of Kenai River kings, it still weighs a solid forty pounds or so, and that is a lot of salmon, especially on fly tackle. A male, he has been in the river long enough to acquire a blush of color on his sides. And now I must decide just what to do with him. There are two distinct choices, and at the risk of stretching the limits of narrative convention I am happy to offer both for the reader's consideration:

Ending A. The fish is in the relatively calm water against the bank at last. I consider the camera safely stowed inside its waterproof bag back in the boat, but the light is dull nothing; a photo would show only dark blobs sillhouetted against a luminous gray river. It is time to say good-bye.

I reach into the pocket of my chest waders and retrieve the hemostat. As the fish glides past my feet, I lean down toward the orange artifact in the corner of his jaw, and when I feel metal on metal, I squeeze and twist quickly and then the fish and I belong to separate worlds once more. The fish is still vigorous and there is no need for resuscitation. He glides away through the shallows, and because the light is so feeble I lose track of him even before he reaches the green water to continue his way upstream.

Ending B. The fish is in the relatively calm water against the bank at last. Suddenly, I realize just how long a winter it has been.

The return of the year's first salmon is a special event. Because of the timing of each species' biorhythms, this honor always falls to the kings. Great feasts once marked the occasion, and while I am not really up to a full-blown potlatch, my friends and I customarily pay annual homage to the concept with a tradition of our own: a backyard get-together with grilled salmon as the main attraction.

What of the catch-and-release ethic, elevated to the status of a covenant with God during this era of politically correct fly-fishing? First, a review of the relevant biology. All Pacific salmon die after spawning, and once a river's escapement goals are met, the addition of more mature fish to the system adds nothing. There is no return of anadromous fish in the world monitored as closely as that of the Kenai River's kings. And while I happen to believe strongly in the catch-and-release philosophy when its merit is proven or even logical, the effect of catch-and-release on mortality among salmon species is largely unknown, and almost certainly not as benign as some naively believe. Who truly has more impact on the resource: the angler who catches one king, quits, and takes it home to dinner, or the enthusiastic visitor who battles dozens to exhaustion and "releases" them to the scavengers downstream? No one really knows, and until we do there is no basis for self-righteousness.

No doubt about it: The salmon finning at my feet is going to feed something. The only question is whether it will be the eagle or my family and friends. I reach down as the eddy cycles my quarry past my feet again and grab his tail. A short wooden club waits among the clutter in the bottom of the boat. Its exercise will be the fulfillment of a covenant too, if not with God, at least with nature. I leave it to others to explain the difference.

So take your pick. I do every time I land one—one king salmon, one trout, one anything. So do you; so do we all. These decisions may be influenced by biology or by social obligation, by hunger or by love. The choice may be easy or it may require soul-searching deliberation. Sometimes we choose beauty and sometimes the beast.

Either way, the idea is to honor properly the big brother who visits us, and as long as we succeed in that, the choice is never wrong.

FOUR

BORN TO KILL

Northern Pike: *Esox lucius*

A MORE PRUDENT INDIVIDUAL probably wouldn't have followed the directions in the first place.

The Quebecois mechanic who gave them to us was friendly enough. We had stopped for gas in a little town on the way to Montreal, where I was about to start my medical internship. Because the station attendant was so expansive, my marginal French felt more fluent than usual. We talked about gas and weather and politics, and before I knew it I was asking him if he knew someplace nearby where we could camp for the night and do some fishing.

His directions, along with the map scrawled on the back of a paper sack with a grease pencil, belonged to the classic annals of you-can't-miss-it mayhem: Turn here, go down this road five miles (or six, or possibly eight), look for the old abandoned truck, turn right just before you get there (or perhaps just after), drive another mile or two until you see a lake on your left, carry the canoe down to the lake, paddle across, look for the big birch tree, portage the canoe one mile due west of there to another little lake no one knows about that is full of huge fish.

"What kind of fish?" it eventually occurred to me to ask.

"Brochet," my informant assured me with a conspiratorial grin as he held his hands apart almost as far as they would go. Pike so big we should carry extra paddles in case they tore the first pair from our hands.

This proposal was just too intriguing to refuse. Montreal and all the responsibility it implied could wait for one more day. We turned where he told us to turn, went down the road five miles (or six, or possibly eight), found the old truck, turned again, and came to a lake. We made camp and Dick and David elected to relax and try fishing right there later that evening. A little voice inside my head told me I should stay there too, but I ignored it. I knew that I could talk Susan into anything then, and sure enough, I could. We carried the canoe down to the water, paddled across to the other side of the lake, found what we hoped was the final landmark, took a compass bearing, and set off across the muskeg.

Alaska's bugs enjoy a reputation as the world's worst, but I can assure you that when it comes to getting eaten alive by insects there is no place quite like eastern Canada. The ground underfoot felt like one vast sponge, and with every footstep mosquitoes emerged like clouds of smoke. We slopped on layer upon layer of repellent, but the sun was still hot and the canoe was heavy and we sweated the bug dope off faster than we could apply it. The little voice was getting louder, but just before it convinced me to turn around I lifted the canoe up off my shoulders and saw the faint sheen of water glimmering somewhere ahead of us through the trees, like a desert mirage. Anyone who has portaged heavy loads through thick forest toward an unknown lake knows what that sight means. It means, among other things, that you cannot possibly turn back until you have sampled the fishing.

Just finding the lake was an obvious triumph, but the bugs were making us too miserable to savor our accomplishment. We rolled the canoe from our shoulders at the water's edge, threw our gear inside, and set out away from shore as fast as we could paddle. Out in the middle of the lake a welcome puff of breeze chased away the mosquitoes at last, and we sat down in the bottom of the canoe, sponged the sweat from our eyes, and felt the lake's cool embrace through the boat's thin aluminum hull with more relief than you can imagine.

We bobbed around lazily until the shadows started to lengthen in the coves, and then it was time to start fishing. I suggested that we rock-paper-scissors for the first shift up front, but Susan volunteered for the stern. We paddled together to the upwind end of the lake and then turned away from the sun so the evening light would be behind us as I cast toward the shore. The line ran easily through the guides of the beat-up glass fly rod. That was all my equipment budget would allow in those days, but somehow it always seemed to get the job done. A piece of heavy mono shock tippet went on the end of the leader, a nondescript streamer went on the end of the shock tippet, and I was fishing at last.

The possibility that there might actually be something to catch in this secret lake of ours was certainly tantalizing, but I knew better than to get my hopes up. For an hour nothing stirred out there in the black water, but it was an idyllic evening anyway. There was just enough breeze to keep the bugs down, but not enough to make casting or paddling a chore. A loon's cry spilled across the lake like quicksilver, and then bats began to appear, feasting on the same bugs that had so recently feasted on us. Susan really didn't have a feel for the water from a fishing perspective, and she wandered away from the shoreline and missed some of the sunken logs and weed beds that I wanted to hit, but I didn't say anything about these minor shortcomings. It was just too mellow an evening for criticism of any kind.

I fished hard in the beginning, making long, ambitious casts and stripping fast because that's what you're supposed to do when trying to catch pike with a fly. By the time we started our second circuit around the lake, however, I wasn't making much of an effort at all. My casting grew lazy, and half the time the streamer simply trolled along behind us. I asked Susan if she wanted to fish and she said she was happy paddling the canoe. I was thinking about what lay ahead of us, on the portage back through the woods in the failing light and then in Montreal and beyond, when the line snubbed up tight somewhere deep in the water between the canoe and the shoreline. The weight on the other end felt so substantial that I assumed the fly had snagged a sunken log.

Then the log began to move and the soporific quality of the evening evaporated in a pulse of adrenaline. I took in line as the fish on the other end ran toward the canoe's midsection like a torpedo and finally passed right beneath us. The urge to look as it came out the other side proved overwhelming, so overwhelming that we almost capsized the canoe in the process. And then we saw it, the malign outline of a huge northern pike retreating toward the deep water, larger than anything either of us could have imagined.

Susan made an inarticulate noise that somehow managed to say it all. I swung the rod around the end of the canoe with the tip down in the water to keep the line from fouling on the rope that trailed from the bow. The fish seemed unimpressed. It did not jump or run, but simply swam away as we followed along in the canoe like a dog on a leash.

The rod was flimsy and the leader full of knots, and there seemed little possibility of landing the fish. We hung on out of fascination, I suppose, the way one might respond to being taken aboard a UFO. The fight itself involved no strategy from either party. The fish just kept on swimming and I just kept on toying with the amount of pressure on the line as Susan paddled us along in whatever direction the pike chose to go. Finally, as if it had taken all the inconvenience it intended to take from us, the pike began to shake its head and roll. It did not seem possible that the leader could survive the savage jerks on the end of the line, but somehow it did. Then the fish turned and began to swim right at the boat again, and it was not at all clear whether this was an offensive or defensive maneuver. At last the pike wound up next to us rolling angrily on the surface, and I knew I had to try to land it. If you were to ask why, I could do no better than to paraphrase Hillary on Everest: I had to land it because it was there.

We didn't have a net and the snag-choked shore offered no place to try beaching the fish. The end game would clearly have to be fought in the middle of the lake. Susan and I discussed our options briefly and then got down in the bottom of the canoe to lower our center of gravity. She stabilized us with the paddle from the stern while I kept pressure on the fish, and when we drifted down on top of it at last I reached over the side and lunged for its gill covers.

At least Susan did her job well, counterbalancing the canoe adroitly enough to keep us from tipping over. And it's not that I didn't try. My hand closed on the pike's massive green head but it was just too big. I dropped the rod and reached with my other hand, nearly capsizing us in the process. For one awkward moment Susan and I slid around the canoe like contestants in a log-rolling contest as the pike's huge oily bulk squirted helplessly through my hands. One good shake of the head was all it needed to snap the leader at last. It stared at us from the surface, panting deliberately through its gill rakers as I stared and panted back. Then it sank slowly into the dark waters from which it had come, leaving us to drift along easily before the last of the breeze and wonder aloud what had happened.

I have met very few individual gamefish about whose weight I was intensely curious, but that was one of them. I'm certain that pike weighed more than thirty pounds, maybe considerably more. And no, it wasn't a muskie. Given the puny leader on the end of my line, that pike might have been some kind of record, not that it would ever have come to that. Decades have passed since then and my perspectives on fishing and other things have changed, but I have almost never wanted to land a fish as badly as I wanted to land that one, which is probably just as well. And there is the fine irony that one of my most memorable encounters came not at the hands of the glamour species examined elsewhere in this volume, but from the often maligned northern pike. Even after countless rainbows and salmon and bonefish, I can still remember the look and feel of that fish. That should tell us something about the nature of glamour if nothing else.

Let's face it: Northern pike look bad—*bad* bad, the way rattlesnakes and black leather jackets and AK-47s look bad. They should. Pike are perfectly designed to fulfill their role in the grand scheme of life, which is to kill other things and eat them, especially other fish.

Of course most gamefish are piscivores, at least when they get big enough to be of real interest. Perhaps it isn't just that northerns kill and devour things that makes us uneasy; perhaps it's the way they go about it.

Consider its appearance. It's always dangerous to examine wildlife from the anthropomorphic perspective, but no fish invites such ideas quite like the pike. One can rationalize that the long, lean, dangerous outline is an obvious product of the function-is-beauty school of design, but you still must come to terms with that face and head: The pouting expression, the undershot jaw, the wicked grin with all those teeth . . . pretty soon we're right in a Hammer Films horror movie. The appearance of northerns conveys evil intentions even though such inferences are biologically ridiculous. A pike's intentions are no more evil than those of a rabbit or a butterfly, all of which simply want to survive and propagate. Nonetheless, a good, close look at a big pike can give you second thoughts about dangling your feet in waters they inhabit.

Then there is the indiscriminate nature of the pike's appetite. When salmonids feed on other vertebrates, they usually show some discretion. Pike, on the other hand, require only that their dinner be alive, and that it fit in their mouth. Or close to it. Ducks, snakes, muskrats, and fish of every description including, yes, other pike have all been recovered from the gullets of northerns. If it can get in the water and move once it's there, old *Esox* stands ready to eat it or choke to death trying.

Pike fishing, for the most part, takes place in markedly different settings than the pursuit of trout and salmon. The water is usually still and warm. And warm, still water in the latitudes inhabited by pike invariably means mosquitoes. Take away the smell of bug dope and the inevitable chorus of whining wings and slapping hands, and I would have trouble believing there were northerns nearby. And there probably wouldn't be.

Technically, fly-fishing for pike is straightforward to a fault. Fly selection? Remember the pike's dietary preferences outlined above. All the fly must do is move, attract attention, and be in the water. It is hard to imagine a fly-fishing tome titled *Selective Pike*. Standard tarpon flies work just fine on northerns, and after saltwater trips I save all my beat-up streamers for this very purpose. While wire leaders enjoy traditional favor among pike fisherman, an eighteen-inch length of forty-pound-test mono gets the job done just as well and is easier to handle and somehow less intimidating than wire, to me if not to the fish.

All of this makes it easy to subscribe to the cynical view that fly-fishing for northerns is nothing more than the tedious pursuit of ugly, second-class fish. Strangely, this opinion is most likely to be encountered among those who have never actually done it. In fact, there is much to admire about the northern pike, despite the nearly complete snub afforded the species in the literature of fly-fishing.

Never mind about the mosquitoes; pike live in wondrous places. There is something compelling about those northwoods lakes, not least of which is that they are seldom crowded. For those who have endured the Big Hole in June and the Kenai in July, there is much to be said for going someplace by yourself and fishing without fanfare once you get there. And pike do fight. They strike hard and make lots of commotion on the surface, and even if their speed and staying power are on the short end of the scale by the standards of most gamefish in this book, they are finally just plain fun.

And then there's variety, that proverbial spice of life. Like a solid diet of truffles, an uninterrupted agenda of bonefish and elegant spring-creek rainbows can become too much of a good thing. Whatever else pike may be on the end of a fly line, they're certainly different.

One summer day a friend and I took his jet boat up a winding Alaska river into the middle of nowhere. We had been fishing for early silvers for two days without finding much but off-color dogs and pinks. The river drained a lake that supported a red salmon run, and we thought we might find some rainbows eating eggs at the mouth of one of the lake's little feeder streams. (And yes, counting the names of all the different gamefish mentioned in this short paragraph *does* make me miss Alaska!)

We found the water at the mouth of the first creek churned to a froth by a school of migrating reds whose path had been arrested by low flow in the spawning stream. The salmon were olive-backed and hook-jawed and I didn't really want to cast out into the chaotic mess they had created, but we had come too far to retreat without firing a shot, so I tied on a streamer and flipped it toward the edge of a nearby weedbed.

Then something struck the fly, and there was an odd quality about the take. The fish wasn't hot enough to be a rainbow, but there was too much head shaking and not enough running for a salmon, even an over-ripe sockeye. The fish sulked around out in the weeds for several minutes before declaring its identity in a display of surface thrashing. Although it was not a very big pike, my friend and I admired it as if we had landed something truly wonderful and exotic.

For the rest of the morning we had a blast drifting around the lake catching northerns in the four- to eight-pound range. We even kept a couple for dinner, and after a summer of all kinds of salmon prepared in all kinds of ways, those deep-fried chunks of pike tasted deliciously different, aggravating little bones and all. Later that summer I told a friend visiting from "Outside" about this encounter and he told me I was crazy. Why, he wondered, would anyone waste a morning catching pike with all those salmon around? And why, for God's sake, would anyone actually eat them? Of course by that point in the season I was almost ready to ask the same two questions about salmon, which just goes to show that excitement is above all else a measure of what you are accustomed to.

My own periodic forays into the obscure world of northern pike typically come at the cost of an opportunity to fish for something else, and so my fascination with this lightly regarded species must have some real substance to it. Perhaps my enjoyment of northerns simply reflects a regard for the places they are found coupled with a need for an occasional break from the salmonids, but I also respect the simple realization that pike are great at what they do. That is a quality I can admire at one level or another in just about anything and anybody. One can imagine some creative force looking at the clear lakes of the pre-Cambrian shield and saying: "What this food chain needs is something at the top!" No design laboratory or computer bank could have come up with anything better suited to this role than the northern pike.

Northerns were born to kill; it's that simple. Predation is their business, and if we all did our jobs as well as pike do theirs, the world would at least be an easier place to predict, if not to understand. Most of the malicious qualities we thoughtlessly ascribe to pike are actually our own malicious qualities reflected and distorted, as by a funhouse mirror. Perhaps after all the bugs have been swatted, that's what pike fishing finally has to teach us.

FIVE

CAPTAIN CLARK'S TROUT

Cutthroat Trout: *Oncorhynchus clarki*

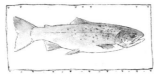

I T IS HARD TO LOOK AT SLOUGH CREEK and not be reminded of all that is wonderful about the Yellowstone ecosystem. The creek's clear water heads high on the Beartooth Plateau and then flows south out of Montana into the park where it joins the Lamar River and eventually the Yellowstone itself. While it tumbles along in places with a life of its own like any high-mountain stream, the creek also knows enough to slow down from time to time and smell the roses, or, more precisely, the sage brush. That unique high-plains combination of crystalline water and sage serves me as a personal definition of the West's great trout fishing. True to form, Slough Creek does not disappoint.

Visit in July and fish the accessible water below the campground and you will find, among other things, plenty of company. Hike upstream to the meadows, on the other hand, and you can still get a taste of the wilderness West, especially in September when the casual tourists have gone home and the hills come alive with the music of bugling elk. Remember that this is still grizzly country, as much as any corner of the lower Forty-Eight. But don't let all these romantic notions distract you too much. Above and beyond all these aesthetic considerations, Slough Creek is one remarkable trout stream.

It's not that you're going to catch huge fish. If trout larger than the benchmark five pounds are important to you, you're in the wrong place. You should head north, head west, head somewhere.

It's not even that you're going to catch a lot of fish, though you certainly might. I have been skunked on Slough Creek. That's right, skunked, as in zero.

Ah, but the fish you do catch. That's the thing: fourteen- to eighteen-inch Yellowstone cutthroats, the most eye-catching strain of an eye-catching species. They don't have to be huge. They don't have to brood like browns or tear up the water like rainbows. These are genuine American originals, and Slough Creek and its environs are meant for those who understand such matters.

I still remember the first Slough Creek cutthroat I caught. It had been a rough morning on the Firehole. After several hours of the kind of fishing that reminds us we aren't as good at this as we think, I set off up the Lamar valley, primarily to do some wildlife photography, not quite sure I ever wanted to see my fly rod again. Slough Creek, however, was an offer I couldn't refuse. Running pure and delicate through the rolling sage-studded terrain, the water seemed to call for something pure and delicate in return, but I had seen enough #20 emergers that day, and since it was the middle of summer and it looked like hopper water, I tied on a deer-hair hopper as thick as my little finger. When I worked the fly out over the water and dropped it up against the opposite bank, the bug hit the surface with such a crash that I thought momentarily of forgetting the whole thing and going home. I fished on up the pool anyway, then suddenly the fly vanished in a slurping take. The fight was dogged and unspectacular but immensely satisfying, because I needed to catch a trout at just that time. The fish that I finally brought into the shallows was just the one I needed, too: a chunky sixteen-inch cutthroat with rich amber sides splattered with spots dark as ink, the crimson slashes beneath its gill covers bright enough to let you know that the cutthroat never could have enjoyed any other popular name.

Oncorhynchus clarki. Scientific names often suggest the elements of a story, and in this case it is the allusion to William Clark that is important. To the astute observer, the name evokes images of discovery and the unique flavor of the American West. Now that the headwaters of the Yellowstone and the Missouri are universally recognized as a world-class trout fishery, it is sometimes hard to realize that those familiar browns and rainbows and brookies are all intruders in the land of wonders encountered by Lewis and Clark, where the cutthroat once was king.

Credit actually goes to Lewis rather than Clark for the first written description of the species. On June 13, 1805, Lewis had this to say about the results of a morning's fishing on the Missouri near what is now Great Falls:

> *Goodrich had caught half a dozen very fine trout . . . These trout (caught in the Falls) are from sixteen to twenty-three inches in length, precisely resemble our mountain or speckled trout in form and the position of their fins, but the specks are of a deep black instead of the red or gold color of those common to the U. States. These are furnished long sharp teeth on the palate and tongue, and generally a small dash of red on each side behind the front ventral fin. The flesh is of a pale yellowish red or, when in good order, of a rose pink.*

How Clark rather than his colleague wound up with his name attached to the fish is not clear, although Lewis's role in the cutthroat's original description is acknowledged in the name of the subspecies that he originally described, *Salmo clarki lewisi.* And what about poor Goodrich? He was probably too busy fishing to worry about his place in scientific history. A man after my own heart.

There are in fact more than a dozen recognized subspecies of cutthroat trout, which should come as no surprise given the huge dimensions and diverse habitat of its historic range. The "west slope" subspecies that wound up bearing Meriwether Lewis's name is actually native to both sides of the Continental Divide, as is the second principal inland variety, the richly colored Yellowstone subspecies represented by my Slough Creek specimen.

None of these variations on the theme is more intriguing than the Lahontan cutthroat, in whose history one can read as much biological triumph and tragedy as one wishes. During the continent's formative glacial epoch, Lake Lahontan occupied much of what is now arid Nevada. This vast body of water allowed its resident trout to evolve into huge, marvelously adapted predators. Pyramid Lake, the modern remnant of that prehistoric body of water, produced the official world-record cutthroat in 1925, a forty-one-pound specimen that is one of the oldest and most secure gamefish records in North America. It is worth remembering that Pyramid Lake was subject to intense commercial-fishing pressure at the end of the last century, and old photographs of fish bound for market in San Francisco suggest that far larger Lahontan cutthroats were taken regularly. God only knows what was swimming around in the depths of Pyramid Lake when Lewis first laid eyes on Goodrich's catch in 1805.

Finally, a series of ill-advised water projects affecting Pyramid Lake and the adjoining Truckee River finished what years of commercial fishing started: the destruction of the finest stocks of Lahontan cutthroats. Water levels fell, temperatures rose, spawners were lost to irrigation ditches, and the alkalinity of the lake increased. By the end of the Second World War, the original strains of Pyramid Lake trout had gone the way of the passenger pigeon. Subsequent stocking and habitat-improvement efforts using trout derived from neighboring waters allowed the reestablishment of a significant cutthroat fishery in the lake, but the best of the genetics were gone forever. The world has seen its last forty-pound cutthroat.

Part of my high regard for anadromous fish stems from a simple fascination with the sea, the source of so much welcome mystery; part comes from the invigorating effect that ocean sojourns have on gamefish, as exemplified by wild steelhead, whose fighting abilities make it one of the few cult objects that deserve its status. As a scientist, I remain fascinated by the twin biological mysteries of anadromous fish: long-distance underwater homing and the physiologic ability to adapt to radically different chemical environments. Any curious observer of the natural world needs to be able to stop fishing long enough to marvel at such things.

It should be no surprise that a western species as widely distributed as the cutthroat comes in a marine version. What is surprising is that the sea-run cut attract so little attention as a gamefish. The problem is largely a matter of competition. In the world of broad-shouldered salmon and steelhead, the anadromous cut is small fry. For those who go down to coastal streams with 8-weight rods and visions of epic battles, it takes a tectonic shift of focus to settle for simple trout fishing, which is what the pursuit of sea-run cutthroat really turns out to be.

One spring day I was standing waist-deep in tidal water on a southeast Alaska stream casting to steelhead that plainly weren't there, an act of atonement that only another steelheader would understand. Finally something picked up my fly as it swept along the gravel bottom. The fish was too small for a jack steelhead but a bit too lively for a Dolly. Soon I was admiring a twelve-inch cutthroat, hardly the fish I had in mind, but clearly an improvement over the steelhead I had not been catching.

I had a 5-weight rod back in the truck, and after a moment's reflection I walked back out to the road and switched gear. For the next two hours I caught sea-run cutthroats. They were spotted vividly in black, although the namesake markings on their gill covers were faint orange at best, as if diluted during their stay at sea. The fish were twelve to fifteen inches long, fought well, and were plentiful and cooperative. As I finally left the stream I asked the obvious question: *Why don't I do this more often?* Then I picked up my steelhead rod and hiked back upriver and spent three more hours casting fruitlessly in the rain, which I suppose in a way answers the question.

I don't like rainbow-cutthroat hybrids. I know that they strike flies and run and jump. I know that they are hardy survivors possessing true hybrid vigor, which endears them to the biologists whose job it is to get trout into places where trout are not. Still, I wish they would go away.

Despite their biological hardiness, I dislike these cutbows, or whatever you want to call them, because they miss the point of both the species from which they are derived. They seem engineered, even though they are one of the only trout hybrids that reproduces naturally in the wild. And I especially dislike them because they'll probably manage to accomplish something that habitat loss and overfishing have so far only threatened: the final destruction of Captain Clark's trout.

For the sad fact is that the cutthroat is a loser—a beautiful loser for certain and a tragic one perhaps, but a loser nonetheless.

From the sportfisher's perspective, the cut is a pushover, just as the species was a pushover for commercial nets in Pyramid Lake a century ago. Fly selection? Toss out a Pale Morning Anything; it'll work on cutthroats. Tagging studies indicate that the average cut in the Buffalo Ford section of the Yellowstone gets caught seven times per season, and some manage the trick every other day. Rocket scientists they are not.

Biologically, the cut is on even shakier ground. They fare terribly in competition with the introduced species that now dominate much of their original range. Browns replaced them easily in the lower reaches of that range soon after their introduction. Conventional wisdom holds that browns adapt more readily to warm water than do cutthroats, but I suspect that the browns simply ate them. In faster, cooler mountain waters, introduced rainbows are loving the cutthroat to death, spawning generations of those hybrids that bother me so much. My dislike for cutbows can be rephrased as blind enthusiasm for cutthroats.

In light of which, let us close on a tumbling mountain stream that must remain anonymous. Unlike Slough Creek, this one will not make anyone's list of Ten Great Western Trout Streams. There may not even be ten people who know there are trout here. which is just fine with me. Some fisheries can tolerate company with ease, but this is not one of them. Here, the solitude itself is the heart of the experience, allowing an intimate and personal relationship with the residents of the stream, fish that might scarcely warrant notice in another setting.

It is September, and the elk are bugling. In fact, it's the elk that got me here in the first place, not that I wouldn't hike this far just to go fishing. The morning is hot and I have hung my bow in the shade back where the tent is pitched. After several hours of being barked at by cows and winded by bulls and generally made a fool, I am ready to match wits with something more my own speed.

Here in the mountains, water always seems to be in a hurry. Today the stream acts as if flowing is a job to be done with enthusiasm. Holding water? Forget it. On streams like this, you often have to hold on yourself just to watch the water go by. Perched on a chunk of granite worn smooth by the current, I study the little slick behind the next boulder upstream. It's hard to imagine a trout lasting there for long, but this is just the sort of water to which the native cutthroat has adapted perfectly.

I choose the fly deliberately: a Royal Wulff, in whose white calf-hair wings I can imagine times when you were not expected to know the scientific name of anything in order to fish with flies, even if you meant to do it well. I may have tied this one thirty years ago. There is little room for improvement upon the pattern anyway, not here on water such as this, where visibility, durability, and buoyancy are more important attributes in a fly than its ability to resemble anything in particular.

There is a trick to this of course, a trick that has nothing to do with 7x tippets and insect trivia. The stream is a riotous cauldron of boils and swirls and cross-currents, and not even a mountain cutthroat will hit a dry fly that looks like it's trying to waterski. The overhanging limbs and treacherous footing don't help either. And so the presentation comes down to balance, flick, and mend, and when the Great White Hope on the end of the leader hits the sweet spot behind the rock, it disappears as if the fish had been waiting for it to arrive all its life.

There will be no screaming reels here on my nameless little trout stream today. The pack rod's flex alone is enough to overwhelm the fish, which soon exhausts itself in a flurry of jerky little runs. I finally guide the trout into the shallows behind me and examine the dark spots and amber sides. Turned over gently in my hand, the deep red slash on the gill covers announces its identity to the world. Free of the Royal Wulff at last, my eight-inch trophy flicks its tail and disappears back into the current.

I'll take another dozen fish before it's time to return to camp, complete my chores, and prepare for the evening bow hunt. The largest will be nine inches long, maybe. Measuring the fish, however, hardly measures the experience of catching them. I find myself hoping selfishly for a cutbow hybrid or two for the simplest of reasons: I would like to kill them and eat them, as a favor to myself and the stream. But these are all true cutthroats, too beautiful to kill, and so my hard-earned lunch eventually consists of nothing but cheese and crackers.

Catching fish like these reminds me of eating pretzels: Each one suggests that you really shouldn't quit until you have had another. The middle of the day passes as easily as a dream. No matter how many times I do this sort of thing, I'm smart enough to know that I never do it enough. I'm no rocket scientist myself, but I can take a certain pride in this bit of insight.

The simple pleasure of catching none-too-bright trout smaller than my hand is tempered by the romantic notion that it probably isn't going to get any better than this. Less than two centuries after its first encounter with our culture, Captain Clark's trout may be little more than a candle in the wind. Despite its remarkable biological diversity, the cutthroat is facing its twilight as a species. Even among the numerous distractions of modern life, we should each be able to find the time to pay our respects. We owe that much to ourselves.

Among others.

SIX

THE FIFTH RESOLUTION

Permit: *Trachinotus falcatus*

I HOPE YOU ENJOYED your thirtieth birthday more than I enjoyed mine.

Susan had just left and I was having trouble adjusting to her absence. Susan is a statuesque woman with long flaming-red hair, a Valkyrie in hip waders, and I never realized how much space she occupied in my life until she was no longer there to occupy it. It had been my fault and I knew it, and so did all of our mutual friends, but it was too late now, and there I was: alone, depressed, and, to top it off, thirty.

That birthday felt like a real milestone anyway, perhaps because when Mario Savio stood on the steps of Berkeley's Sproul Hall and made his 60's Zeitgeist proclamation about never trusting anyone over thirty, I had been there. It seemed like a good idea at the time, and it still did. To tell the truth, it still sounds like a good idea, despite its personal implications.

What friends remained after my pointless and final falling-out with Susan were not about to let the occasion pass unnoticed. Since my birthday occurs in June, I honestly would have preferred to be down at the creek working out the first of the real summer caddis-fly hatches, but I had pissed off enough people already, so I stayed home and let the party happen to me. There wasn't much to it really, just some beer and rock 'n' roll and generic edginess between me and one or two of the unattached women, but by the time the inevitable cake appeared I was tired of everything, so I walked out the back door and disappeared into the night with the dog.

He was a yellow Labrador retriever. His name started off as Skykomish Sunrise in honor of the steelhead fly, but the AKC informed me that there was already a Lab registered under that name (believe it or not), so he became Skykomish Sunka Zee instead. *Sunka Zee* is Sioux for yellow dog, so I suppose that the name was something of a tautology if you speak Sioux, but not many people do. Even when I still lived on the reservation, hardly anyone got it, although occasionally one of the older women would cackle in delight when I mentioned the dog's name. One thing was certain: He was the best dog I ever had, and at the risk of insulting one or two people, he's right in the running for being the best friend I ever had as well.

So we left the noise and confusion behind and headed off on our own. We went all the way down to the creek, where I sat on the bank and listened to the water gurgle past and the trout smack caddis flies while I groped around for emotional bearings. My life felt short on direction, and my thirtieth birthday seemed like an opportune time to address this deficiency. I leaned back in the grass and looked up at the summer sky, and by the time the fish stopped rising in the nearest pool I had made a list of five goals to accomplish by the time I was thirty-five. Lists like this invite argument, but I was happy with my choices, and I still am. With Skykomish Sunka Zee as my witness, I promised that within the next five years I would:

1. Learn to fly.
2. Shoot a sheep.
3. Publish a work of fiction.
4. Run a marathon.
5. Catch a permit on a fly.

Until now, I never told anyone about any of this except the dog.

I saw my first permit that winter, before I had even gotten around to thinking seriously about the Five Lofty Goals.

We ran for an hour out behind the village that morning. We were early and a faint layer of haze hung over the water, so when Pete cut the motor there was nothing to do at first but drift along with the tide and wait for the light.

Belize was different then. It had not yet become a destination for the young and the restless, and there was still a certain anonymity associated with being an American there, an easiness of spirit that would not survive the eventual onslaught by my sometimes embarrassing countrymen. Ambergris Cay was a wonderful place to catch small bonefish and medium-size tarpon, and we were intent upon the latter that morning as we studied the vast flat stretching away in all directions toward the undefined horizon.

Ahead of the boat a manatee's roily wake cut through the marl and disappeared into the haze, and Pete studied it longingly. He had already confessed his desire to harvest a manatee for food, but, well developed as they were, I didn't know if my own hunter-gatherer instincts went quite that far. I tried to imagine what it would be like to track down a sea cow and sink a harpoon into it, and suddenly it seemed like a good time to establish an interest in fishing, despite the marginal light. I tied a streamer onto the shock tippet and climbed onto the bow. Pete's setup wasn't fancy, just a fourteen-foot skiff with an outboard and a cooler full of lunch. The boat lacked a formal casting platform and most of the other accoutrements of high-brow flats fishing. When we got into fish I had to watch my loose line carefully, what with all the obstructions lying around on deck, but that was a small price to pay for the relaxed ambiance of Pete's skiff.

Finally Pete began to pole while I stood high and alone in the bow and stared out into the amorphous expanse of air and water. There was something hypnotic about the rhythm of the waves against the boat and the utter lack of visual figure-ground reference ahead, and within a matter of minutes I felt lost. I was concentrating on the search for tarpon, and because I was searching for their long, reptilian shapes the permit's appearance caught me by surprise.

The tail showed first, as it often does. The twin projections formed by the superior lobe of the tail and the dorsal fin of a permit feeding in the shallows are often visible at some distance. We were in deeper water though, and that's another matter entirely. The black, scimitar-shaped outline of the tail just appeared in front of me, undulating, surreal, and disembodied, more like a presence summoned forth at a séance than part of a fish. "Permit!" Pete hissed from the stern, and then I finally saw the rest of it, the dark penciled outline of its fins and the silver-green mirage of its flanks as it tacked back and forth above the marl.

There was no time to change flies, and nothing to do but marvel at the fish and salute it by casting the gaudy tarpon streamer in its direction, which I did. To my amazement, the permit spun around and began to follow the grotesque orange collection of feathers as I stripped the line nervously back toward the boat. Just as it seemed that the impossible was about to occur in a definitive display of beginner's luck, the fish veered away and disappeared from my life as effortlessly as it had arrived.

"Big one!" Pete said from the stern as I stared at the empty ocean and tried to adjust to reality.

"Did you *see* that?" I said. "He almost took the tarpon fly!"

"Big one!" Pete repeated, and why not? That's always a handy phrase to fill in the blanks after remarkable encounters with fish.

I went on talking, to Pete, to the sea, to myself, about the closeness of the encounter, how the permit in all its glory had been that close to inhaling the improbable offering. The unstated thesis, of course, was that if I had really been prepared, with a reasonable leader and what passed then for a permit fly, the most difficult of my five resolutions would have been a done deal.

Little did I realize how naïve all this would sound to anyone experienced in the quixotic quest for a permit on a fly.

Permit are not meant to be caught on flies. I know this for a fact: Over the years, countless dozens of them have told me so.

Among serious fly-fishers, taking a permit is akin to sighting the Abominable Snowman: Rumors persist, but doing it yourself is very much another matter. Permit would be far easier to come to terms with if the last one-half of one percent of them did what all the others do and refused the fly. Unfortunately, there is irrefutable evidence that it can be done.

Permit would also be less problematic if they were just another gamefish. In fact, they would be a compelling quarry even without all that permit-on-a-fly hype. No other fish is as visually compelling as a permit, with the dramatic dark outline of its fins and tail, its ghostly iridescence, and the way it swims—like a nervous, athletic predator—all of which reminds me of UFO sightings: strange shapes glowing weirdly and moving without regard for the laws of physics.

And when you *hook* one, well. . . . Survivors of such events babble on about them at socially inappropriate moments for the rest of their lives, like unreconciled Elvis fans or returnees from out-of-body experiences—clearly changed, though not necessarily for the better. Some even regard landing a permit on a fly as a perfect excuse to stop fishing. One imagines them weeping, like Alexander, because there are no more worlds to conquer. Some pace and fidget pathetically, like junkies waiting for their man, while others stare off into space like surfers searching for the perfect wave—even when there is no ocean nearby. Many disappear without explanation at odd times of the year only to return wearing suntans and detached, conspiratorial looks. It seems that no experience will ever again be as invigorating as catching a permit on a fly, or catching another permit on a fly, or another—all of which serves to define a peculiar sort of misery known only by the doomed.

Clearly this is a fish to be reckoned with.

The air felt hot enough to melt flesh. The sea was still and empty and the equatorial sun hovered straight overhead like a vulture. Alone on foot, with nothing but water and sand visible in all directions, I had spent the morning fishing downwind across the most expansive and intimidating reach of saltwater flats I know. The bonefish had been feeding toward me into the wind all morning, and I caught so many of them that I gave up casting to all but the largest. Now it was time to study the glimmering mirage of sand and sea for landmarks, for if I did not correctly identify the one spit in the middle of the lagoon that the truck could drive to, I would spend the night here.

When I thought that I had my bearings at last, I slogged on across another half mile of coral to a bluewater channel that I would clearly have to swim. Plenty of sharks had haunted the edges of the flats that morning, and as I studied the cut in front of me, the route they took to the shallows became painfully obvious. As I removed the surgical scrub pants that I always wear on the flats for sun protection and stuffed them into my belly bag in preparation for the swim, I began humming an ominous progression of dissonant notes that I finally recognized as the theme from *Jaws*.

Which is why I jumped when the fish appeared suddenly and literally out of the blue. Even in the shallows sharks often leave me hysterically hopping up and down, trying to get out of the water by climbing trees that are not there. When I finally got my emergency systems under control and took a good look at the fish, I saw the iridescent flash of color, the flat sides, the crescent tail. My God, it was huge.

There was no time to do anything but cast reflexively with the fly already on the leader, which happened to be a standard bonefish pattern of some kind. The fish was across the wind by this time, so I led and hoped and whipped the line out like a pitcher getting everything possible behind a fastball. The fly plopped down inelegantly on the fish's head and the water swirled beneath it, but instead of disappearing into the security of the channel, the fish attacked the fly so savagely I don't know how the tippet survived. My God, I said again as the line began to melt off the reel spool.

And that is pretty much what you should be saying to yourself at this point in the narrative, at least if you have bought into the permit-on-a-fly program, whether by virtue of prior experience or what you have read here. The problem is that I've been less than candid with you for several paragraphs in a row. Oh, everything described took place all right. It's just that the setting was not the Caribbean but the mid-Pacific, and the fish tearing me to pieces was not a permit but a giant trevally.

The two species certainly have plenty in common. They're both members of the Jack family and share many physical characteristics. While the trevally (or *ulua* as it is known to Hawaiians, a name I prefer because of its beautiful phonetic resonance and personal association with sushi bars) is something more of a deepwater species, it certainly makes guest appearances on the flats where it can be stalked with the fly. Only upon issues of temperament do the *ulua* and the permit part company in earnest.

The day before my hookup in the lagoon, the trevally had given us an object lesson in their character in the deep water beyond Christmas

Island's barrier reef, where I caught an eighty-pounder on rod and reel without benefit of any hooks.

Of course that claim warrants some explanation. Ray and Sheli and I all wanted to catch a big trevally on a fly, and we decided that the way to do it would be to coax them up from the reef with a teaser plug so that we could cast to them on the surface. I borrowed a baitcasting rod from someone in camp and removed the hooks from an old surface plug that had ridden around in my saltwater junk box for decades. Later that morning we took one of the lagoon punts out to the reef, and Ray and Sheli stood at port arms with their fly rods while I began to make long downwind casts with the teaser. Suddenly a dark shape detached itself from the rocks and rocketed toward the plug. "Here he comes!" I shouted unnecessarily as I ground at the reel and skipped the plug back toward the boat as fast as possible, which proved not to be fast enough. The rod tip went down hard as the fish smashed the hook-less wooden plug and sounded, and then there was nothing left to do but ignore the fundamental absurdity of the situation and fight the fish.

Even with fairly heavy tackle it took nearly half an hour to pump the *ulua* to boatside. We all expected to find the fish wrapped up in the line somehow, but it wasn't. The plug was clenched firmly but freely between the fish's jaws as if it had caught its dinner and wasn't letting go, no matter what. As the *ulua* arrived beside the boat I couldn't help comparing it to a permit, so similar in appearance and so profoundly dissimilar in attitude. Then we all enjoyed a collective shrug of the shoulders at the elusive meaning of it all, the fish went into the ice chest for sashimi, and we went back to the drawing board in search of another plan with which to take a giant trevally on a fly.

And what about the one I hooked on the bonefish fly at the edge of the bluewater channel the following day? It broke off, of course. Although only half the size of the specimen taken on the teaser plug, it still packed way too much punch for any bonefish leader in existence. It offered one wonderful screaming run before we parted company, during the course of which I found myself oddly distracted by thoughts of permit. "So this is what it's like," I said to myself, suddenly aware of why those who have done it seem so universally obsessed with the idea of doing it again, a response reliably evoked by only one or two other entries on the menu of human experience. It was as if the *ulua* had been put there to mock deliberately the whole permit-on-a-fly idea. Like some naïve country cousin, the trevally was so easy while the permit itself remained so maddeningly difficult. *Why couldn't it be the other way around?* I wondered briefly as I stared out across the reaches of the sultry sea, and then the answer to my own question became clear. If it *were* the other way around, we would all be obsessed with *ulua* and would laugh about breaking off permit.

With that realization firmly in place, I reeled in the last of the line and readied myself once again for the swim across the channel and all its contents.

It is early in the morning here in the outer reaches of the Turneffe Islands, and I'm almost thirty-five years old.

The sun is still low over the ocean and the light is not conventionally favorable for sight-casting, but I have discovered something wonderful and new to add to my list of tricks when it comes to seeing game while fly-fishing in salt water. As the waves rise just outside the reef and prepare to wash up onto the ocean flat, the morning sun shines right through them from behind, and with a little practice it's actually possible to see fish suspended there like bubbles in a cube of ice. Schools of bones wait in the surf to ride up onto the flat, but they don't interest me. This morning I'm fishing with the sort of intensity that does not allow for distractions.

In the going on five years since my seminal midnight walk along the creek, I have learned the way of the air, published, and shot the sheep. Skykomish, for his part, has retired gracefully to the hearth, where he derives a certain grim satisfaction from my futile efforts to groom one of several unruly pups into a proper replacement. That leaves permit and a marathon, a no-brainer of a choice if ever there was one.

And we saw them there yesterday, working the surf on the same tide. Actually, *I* saw the fish; Blind Bonefish Earl, as Ray and I have rechristened our intrepid guide, didn't see much of anything. The discovery that one's bonefish guide cannot see fish even when they're swarming about his ankles might be regarded with alarm in some circles, blindness ordinarily being a fairly serious liability in a sport that depends above all else upon visual acuity. But I have been at this long enough that I really don't need help seeing fish, and Earl is unfailingly good company, so we're slogging along happily through the surge in a marvelous state of mutual tolerance.

I point to the wave in front of us where a pair of five-pound bones are rising and falling with the sea. "Boxfish," Earl announces with authority.

"By God it is," I agree, because I like Earl so much I just can't help it.

"Two of them, mon," he chides with a laugh.

I'm being a bit unfair to Earl. In two days of fishing with him here in the Turneffes, I have learned that his nearly complete inability to see fish in the water is at least partly compensated for by an uncanny ability to see *tailing* fish at great distances. It's a curious marriage of strengths and weaknesses, and I find myself wishing I could get Earl to one of my eye doctor friends to see if this problem could be fixed with drops or glasses or something. Meanwhile, Earl is good for company and tailing fish and not much else.

Then suddenly and improbably Earl is on-point beside me, sighting up the beach along his extended arm. "Permit!" he hisses. I know from experience that I must look above the water, and when I shift my view I finally see what he has seen: the matched dark filaments of a permit's tail and dorsal fin as the fish works the water rising and falling onto the beach forty yards ahead.

I ease the fly free from the cork butt and begin to work out line, crouching low to the water and stalking toward the fish. The permit continues to advance and retreat from the sandy flat with each rise and fall of the surge, as if its terrain-following guidance system is programmed to keep it in one constant water depth wherever that should take it. The sea looks like beer as it breaks behind the reef, and when the fish submerges I cannot see it, but somehow the twin antennae always reappear to mark its way. The fish is active and intent, and I am overcome with the premonition that if I do everything just right I'm going to hook it.

The breeze is coming in straight and hard from the ocean, leaving me with a crosswind cast made all the more difficult by the faulty aerodynamics of my new permit fly. Because I have gotten painfully serious about all this, I am no longer content to whang away at permit with whatever bonefish or tarpon pattern happens to be on the end of the line when the fish finally makes its appearance. Over the winter, I have experimented at the tying bench with several patterns designed to imitate the crabs that comprise the permit's preferred food. In years to come, better practitioners of the art will devise all sorts of variations on the same theme, culminating in the exquisite and highly functional McCrab, but now the unruly glob of hair and feathers and lead whistling by overhead can pass for genuine innovation. I call it the Blue Crab Special, and in a high wind it is nothing to be trifled with.

In range at last, I fix the permit's position on an incoming wave, double-haul, and feel the line foul improbably behind my right shoulder on something that isn't supposed to be there. I swear and turn and there is Blind Bonefish Earl, who has blundered up behind me and now stands there looking perplexed, the Blue Crab Special hanging from his earlobe like costume jewelry.

Fortunately, this becomes Earl's finest hour. Without missing a beat he reaches up, runs the leader into his mouth, and bites it in two. "Keep your eye on the fish!" he hisses between his teeth as he reaches into the belly bag and retrieves another Blue Crab Special. I study the foam for the permit's tail and relocate it just as Earl finishes tying the second fly to the leader. "Cast, mon!" he urges, retreating cautiously upwind.

It's not a bad cast. In fact, considering the wind and the distance and the bulk on the end of the leader, it's a pretty good one. The Blue Crab Special plops into the suds just ahead of the permit. I let it settle and twitch it back with my line hand, and when it hesitates I lift the rod tip, fully expecting to find that I have accomplished nothing more exciting than foul-hooking the coral bottom. But the resistance on the other end feels soft and sensual, and then the rod tip bucks and I realize that the impossible has actually happened.

The surprise is so overwhelming that I never really set the hook properly; in a matter of seconds the fish turns and heads toward the edge of the reef, and our encounter is over. Earl says nothing. I say nothing.

I reel in the lifeless line and the Blue Crab Special follows like a rag doll trying to surf. When I finally turn and look at Earl there is nothing left to do but laugh. I'm laughing at him because he has a fly for an earring, and I imagine that he's laughing at me because I just blew a shot at a twenty-pound permit. Whatever the case, a good measure of laughter seems to be just what the morning needs. Earl gamely suggests that we fish on down the beach, but I point out that a 2/0 hook impaled in one's ear is nothing to ignore indefinitely.

As we turn and slog back toward the skiff and the long run home toward my surgical kit, the waves continue to rise and fall just beyond the reef and I imagine the face of God peeking back at me from every one of them.

So here I am, fifteen years down the road from my thirtieth birthday and all those lofty promises, and I never have caught a permit on a fly, or on anything else for that matter. I never ran the marathon either, a failure due purely to laziness driven by the realization that I would rather spend my summers fishing than running. Maybe I ought to feel bad about that lack of resolve, but I never quite get around to that. Goals are fine things, but they should never be allowed to ruin your life, especially if they prevent you from going fishing.

In the case of the permit, I can at least hold my head high. I tried, and at the risk of serving up what sounds like something of a rationalization, it seems that the trying may be what is really important about this. I do not need to weep like Alexander; I've got enough problems. There should always be something out there that remains supremely hard to catch, and as long as there are permit in the sea, there most certainly will be.

SEVEN

HUMPIES FROM HELL

Pink Salmon: *Oncorhynchus gorbuscha*

THE TEA-COLORED WATER of the remote southeast Alaska river gathered itself against the opposite bank, raced through a scattering of boulders, and finally spilled down into the head of the pool in which I stood. Downstream, the tide had turned and the water was starting to fall away once again toward the gray Pacific. After the inevitable fumbling courtesy of anticipation and cold fingers, I slid a knot down onto the streamer's eye and forged my way deeper into the pool, anxious to see just what the last tide had brought into the stream.

The first few casts were simply measures of distance and drift, but the streamer soon found the sweet spot just above the gravel bottom that meant I was salmon fishing at last. Overhead, the sun started to break through the inevitable coastal clouds, but the heart of the run still lay in deep shadows cast by the conifers towering above the opposite bank. I couldn't really see what I was fishing to, and for the moment the pool's contents remained a mystery. The fly could have been sweeping past schools of fresh silvers or nothing more than a few resident Dollies. This element of the unknown lends a certain intrigue to the pursuit of anadromous fish, however, even if it is something of an acquired taste. Trout waters offer their own sort of unpredictability, but at least you know in a general sense that the fish are *there*. Salmon streams, on the other hand, can be teeming with fish one day and barren the next. While sight-casting to salmon or steelhead has an appeal of its own, there is nothing quite like a sudden strike as a fly drifts through a dark and brooding pool to affirm one's faith in nature, and possibly in one's self.

A dozen casts into my exploration of this run, that is exactly what took place. The line simply hesitated for an instant, defying the laws of hydraulic flow. My strike was pure reflex, the product of a misspent youth on the steelhead streams of Washington state. The fish bucked, ran, and finally broke water over in the shadows, revealing nothing but a faint glimmer in the darkness. With my light tackle, it took several minutes to work the fish into the illuminated shallows on my own side of the stream, where its arced contour and leopard-spotted back at last identified it as a pink salmon.

Suddenly, the tail of the pool came alive with rolling fish. No one really knows why migrating Pacific salmon surface in stereotyped fashion, but legions of frustrated anglers have proved over the years that they aren't feeding on something that can be imitated by a fly. My own theory, based on nothing other than my imagination, is that they're somehow keying off the angle of the sun to facilitate the homing process, itself another mystery of the genus *Oncorhynchus*. The form these surface antics take is a virtual signature of each salmon species, and the fish invading my pool were unquestionably pinks.

I brought my bellwether fish, a bright five-pound male, into ankle-deep water and released him. By the time I had regrouped and waded back into the current, his buddies had taken over the pool like a street mob. The stream's once calm surface boiled, and fish slapped against my waders in the shallows. I lost all hope of hooking any silvers, my original quarry that morning. Quietly, I watched the fish that I had just released recover and fin his way back into the flow to join the riot. Then I collected my bedraggled streamer and set off upriver, wondering about the prejudices that can lead an angler to abandon a pool full of sporty, cooperative salmon just because they aren't quite the kind of salmon he had in mind.

This scene took place in southeast Alaska while I was in pursuit of fresh coho, but it might just as easily have happened to an angler intent on trophy rainbows in some Bristol Bay drainage. No matter where sportfishermen encounter them, pink salmon quickly manage to wear out their welcome. Pinks tend to overwhelm by sheer numbers even as their Quasimodo profiles offend the sensibilities of anglers intent on streamlined mint-bright fish. Instead of enjoying all the things these fine little salmon really have to offer, fly-fishers all too often dismiss them out of hand. I'll admit that I've sworn at them a time or two myself, and in the middle of a genuine pink salmon invasion it's easy to start imagining the titles of vintage science fiction thrillers: They Came from the North Pacific . . . the Return of the Humpies from Hell!

This reaction is sometimes understandable, but seldom entirely fair.

Of all the Pacific salmon, the pink stands out at once by virtue of both its numbers (the most) and its size (the smallest). As a kid fishing the waters of Puget Sound, I certainly ran into pinks from time to time. These encounters were strictly incidental to the pursuit of silvers and were generally dismissed with nothing more than a casual note of surprise. I never really appreciated how many pink salmon there are in the world until I moved to Alaska. One day soon after my arrival, I found myself skirting the shore of Prince William Sound in my Super Cub scouting for goats in anticipation of an upcoming bow hunt. Each tiny creek that I passed had a dark-brown stain spreading from its mouth out to sea. As I dropped down for a closer look, I finally realized that these discolorations were actually schools of fish. A quick beach landing and a couple of double-hauls later, I learned that the fish were all pinks. The creeks were so small and the fish so numerous that it seemed physically impossible for the fresh water to accommodate all of them. Even in a land of superlatives, the sight of all those fish lining up to fight their way upstream to spawn remains unforgettable. I doubt that I ever wanted to do anything so badly, even that.

Those same beaches, of course, have since been fouled by crude oil. While the long-term effects of the Exxon *Valdez* disaster remain unknown, strong pink salmon runs have been recorded even since the spill. In fact, 1991 saw such strong pink returns in Prince William Sound as a result of fisheries enhancement programs that Alaskans were faced with a unique problem in wildlife biology: too many fish. Historically, the commercial catch of pinks from the Prince William Sound and Southeast Alaska districts has provided the most bountiful salmon harvests in the state, serving up fish literally by the millions for canneries and processors. While it is never safe to be complacent about the future, there are a *lot* of pink salmon out there; so many, in fact, that even human stupidity at its absolute worst couldn't make much of a dent in their numbers.

From the standpoint of the pink's reputation among sport fishers, that abundance is actually part of the problem. Pinks are plentiful to a fault. They do not enter freshwater streams so much as they invade them. Under the clear water conditions that usually prevail in the short drainages favored by humpies, the angler sometimes has to endure the frustration of watching a fly drift past hundreds of mouths before getting a strike. Their sheer numbers often make it difficult to fish selectively for other species. Familiarity really does breed contempt, and when the pinks are in the rivers in force, that is all too often how fly-fishers regard them.

The pink's prestige as a sport fish also suffers from certain peculiarities of its lifestyle and natural history. Humpies do everything just a little bit faster than other salmon. Their brief two-year life cycle is shorter than that of any other Pacific species. This two-year reproductive periodicity, by the way, means that many streams show marked variations in pink returns between odd- and even-numbered years, with distinct populations that hardly overlap at all. Genetic mixing depends on the fact that pinks are less accurate homers than other salmon, and often wind up in the wrong place entirely. When they do return to their native streams to spawn, they enter fresh water like commandos with a mission and a strict schedule. Well adapted to southern Alaska's short, steep coastal drainages, pinks mature rapidly in fresh water and spawn without delay, often right in their home stream's intertidal zone. All this means that by the time pinks come within range of freshwater anglers, they're often starting to look generously ripe. To the experienced, who properly equate the sporting quality of anadromous fish with their freshness from the sea, this trait is at the least an aesthetic liability. Even vigorous males demonstrate a characteristic hump by the time they reach fresh water, and once they start upstream the transformation from fighter to spawner is remarkably rapid. Sheer dead weight on the end of a fly line, spawning pinks with their contorted profiles, dark coloration, and snaggletoothed kypes hardly inspire sporting enthusiasm. Humpies from Hell indeed.

With all this on the record, it might seem easy to dismiss the pink salmon as a sportfish. Certainly there are those who would do just that. But the real point to be made is that fresh pink salmon, taken at an appropriate time on appropriate tackle, are a fine challenge to the fly-fisher. They strike flies readily, as readily as any of the other Pacific salmon species. They run and jump and make reels sing, and otherwise do all the things a fish can be expected to do on the end of a fly line. And when ocean-fresh, they're even attractive: sleek, lean, and heavily spotted along the back, as much as anyone could ask for in a fish of that size.

Fly selection for pink salmon is hardly an exact science. At times, all migrating salmon can be finicky to the point of exasperation, pinks included. Move a few miles up- or downriver and they'll hit, well, anything. I admit that I have never taken a pink salmon on a #20 Blue Winged Olive, but I have no doubt that this could be done with enough effort. Any bright fly that sinks is a genuine pink salmon pattern. I have taken pinks on bucktails, Muddlers, Woolly Worms, bonefish flies, and egg patterns. On one occasion when I was amusing myself by coaxing grayling to the surface through schools of pinks, I became convinced that humpies will hit dry flies, although I certainly wouldn't recommend this to anyone who really needed to catch a fish. At any rate, selectivity is certainly not part of the pink's sporting profile.

Pinks are often taken incidentally by anglers who are after other fish. Since the other fish in question are often silver salmon, pinks frequently wind up being caught on fly tackle in the 8-weight range, and therein lies another part of the problem. The pink's lightweight reputation in sporting circles derives in part from the simple fact that the pink *is* a lightweight, at least by salmon standards, and one that is often taken on gear meant for larger game. Those willing to fish for them with rods really appropriate to four-pound fish will find themselves enjoying a whole new perspective on the diminutive humpy. Streams are usually low and clear during typical August pink runs, and large, heavily weighted flies are seldom necessary. All this means that a floating 5-weight line is adequate for the job, and tackle in this class certainly allows the sporty little pink a fuller expression of its character.

Pinks in salt water offer another fly-rod opportunity that shouldn't be overlooked. The Prince William Sound scene described earlier is hardly unusual. Pinks mill about for some time before they enter fresh water, and they're often within range of shore when they do. While casting distances are usually more demanding in salt water, beaches offer lots of room to maneuver, and ocean-bright salmon always represent their species at its best. I've spent many August mornings casting to pinks in the salt, and the combination of coastal scenery and fast action on the fly rod is the sort of thing that lingers in the memory no matter what salmon species is involved.

No discussion of the humpy would be complete without mention of its value to the beginning fly-fisher. If I were to design a fish for the sole purpose of introducing kids to the pleasures of the fly rod, I would be hard-pressed to improve on the pink salmon. Pinks are plentiful, cooperative, and vastly forgiving. Large enough to provide some real zip on the end of a line, they are still manageable for a beginner, even on light tackle. And when you're in the right place at the right time, they just keep coming at you. Watching my own kids flail away at pinks has given me hours of pleasure, just as it has made them better at the game. And just to be certain that we're not getting too snooty about all this, I would note that the childish delight a river full of pinks can provide is there for veterans to enjoy as well. Let us all remember, please: Catching fish on flies is supposed to be fun.

"Those can't all be fish!" Joe exclaims, as my son, Nick, studies the water with a knowing smile. The boys are twelve years old. Joe has never been to Alaska before, while Nick, who grew up here, can savor the inside knowledge of his early childhood experience. I am reminded once again that there is no way to reproduce the pleasures of a favorite slice of the outdoors quite like experiencing it again through the eyes of your kids.

Ray and I and the two boys are standing on a high bank overlooking a small coastal Alaska stream. The rain forest rises at our backs while the cold Pacific lies in wait several hundred yards around the bend in front of us. In the clear water below, a seething mass of dark shapes turns, ebbing and flowing with the current. They are indeed fish, Joe's disbelief notwithstanding. I can occasionally distinguish the irregularly colored backs of dog salmon, and it's nice to hope that there are silvers down there somewhere, but for the most part these are pinks, all five thousand of them. Ray and I send the boys down the bank with their fly rods while we sit down on a log to watch the show.

Despite a week's worth of preparatory lectures about the need to keep dry things dry, both kids are immediately in over their waders. No matter; you can do things like that when you're twelve years old. Streamers whistle through the air as the boys make up for their technical shortcomings with limitless enthusiasm. The pinks are taking and within minutes both rods are bent double. Of the four of us, it is impossible to tell who is having the most fun.

The boys land these fish, release them, cast again. Salmon stir and move upriver. More arrive to take their place. A sudden splash shatters the pool's clear surface as one of the kids hooks another fish. From my elevated vantage, it seems as if he has hooked them all as the school shifts its weight around to accommodate the disturbance. Downriver, a black bear appears, stares at us briefly, then goes about its business at the streamside. Overhead, an eagle settles into a tree, waiting patiently, as if it has all the time in the world.

I have my fishing gear and my camera, and for a moment it seems that I really ought to *do* something. The fact is that the kids are having so much fun down there catching fish and I'm having so much fun up here watching them that it's hard to imagine a course of action that would improve upon anyone's enjoyment of the day.

A few years ago, a friend endured a shoot-out of a divorce. In her petition to the court, his soon-to-be-ex accused him of neglecting the marriage for the pursuit of "unnecessary fun." (Read hunting and fishing.) What a marvelous philosophical dilemma that phrase poses. Now I find myself wondering if there can really be such a thing. Under what circumstances does fun become unnecessary? What is going on down there in the river seems entirely necessary to me.

It is just the afternoon to ponder such questions. Never mind that two years later I will be subject to similar accusations when I separate from Nick's mother; such unpleasantness is unimaginable on an afternoon like this one. Now salmon move upriver and the boys fish on while I settle back in the sun. Today, like the eagle, I seem to have all the time in the world.

Thanks to the Humpies from Hell.

Of course, it's not possible to make a legendary fish out of the proverbial sow's ear. Pink salmon do swim upstream in hordes, turn into humpbacked monsters, and fill the Pacific air with the smell of decay when their spawning run is over, but then our species has its own uncouth habits. And yes, if you're trying to coax a trophy silver or rainbow from a stream that has been invaded by humpies, it's all too easy to get tired of them. Pinks aren't silvers or rainbows and we might as well accept that from the beginning. Rather than trying to force the issue, perhaps the pink salmon run should be a time to set the fly rod aside for a moment and consider the larger sense of things, for the force of life is seldom more apparent than it is on an Alaska river choked with salmon obeying their instincts. And if you are really willing to address the pink on proper terms, there will come a time, somewhere down near the tide line when you're using light tackle appropriate to the fish, when those Humpies from Hell may give you all that you might ask of them and perhaps a little more.

All of us should be so lucky.

EIGHT

HELLO, DOLLY

Dolly Varden: *Salvelinus malma*

N YET," OUR RUSSIAN FRIENDS responded emphatically to our eager questions about the possibility of fish in the nearly ice-bound river. They were certain it would be barren. We were too far north for the unique Asiatic cherry salmon and it was too early in the season for *nerka,* our own familiar sockeye. Fishing was a largely incidental activity on this particular late spring excursion into the vast Siberian wilderness, so there was no reason to be upset by their gloomy verdict other than the most important reason of all: I wanted to go fishing.

Having spent several weeks in the Russian bush during the preceding year, however, we had learned a thing or two about the chronic pessimism of our hosts. Simply put, no one envisions hopelessness quite as predictably as a Russian; whether this is the cause or the effect of their difficult history is open to speculation. Because we had yet to hear our friends sound enthusiastic about the possibility of fish even when rivers were plainly stuffed with them, we ignored their pained looks, dug our survival fly-fishing gear out of our duffel bags, and headed for the water. I couldn't imagine a stream as attractive as this one being barren, and I still can't.

After several seconds of intense deliberation I selected one of the green-and-white bucktails that years of experience with anadromous fish of all persuasions have made a prominent feature of my basic wilderness fly book. We were only a few miles from the tide line; whatever was waiting out in the current had probably spent some time recently in the North Pacific. With nothing but instinct to serve as a guide, the gaudy streamer seemed a reasonable place to start.

The Russians' gloomy predictions did not survive the first cast. As the fly arced through the last few degrees of its maiden drift, the line hesitated and I struck back at something solid and substantial. After the fish made several brief, dogged runs, I shamelessly horsed it into the shallows, motivated above all else by a desire to learn just what was on the end of the line. Bright as a new chrome fender, the sleek six-pound fish was nearly devoid of markings and coloration, but its predatory outline identified it immediately as a sea-run Dolly Varden.

The fish turned out to be only the first of many. Alaska veterans will recognize the lack of hyperbole in a fish-with-every-cast description of the next hour's events; others will just have to take my word for it. Fresh from the sea, the Dollies fought as hard as char are ever likely to fight. They ranged in size from two to eight pounds and were more than vigorous enough to keep us busy on our minimalist tackle. When we finally returned to camp, we found the Russians settling into a typical evening meal of ominous soup and vodka. They greeted us with a flurry of good cheer and amused Russian. "How many did you catch?" Andrei interpreted with a wry smile.

"About forty," I replied.

"Well, where are they?" the hungry crew demanded.

"We threw them all back," I explained.

Skeptical laughter greeted this announcement, followed by another flurry of Russian that required no formal translation. Hilarious was the tale of the crazy Americans who went to a river with nothing in it, armed only with hooks and feathers, and who then claimed to have caught forty fish in an hour—only to throw them all back into the water. Vodka all around!

After which, the soup didn't taste bad at all.

From one corner of the Pacific rim to the other, I have lost track of the number of times Dolly Vardens have saved the day. They have filled in the blanks between salmon runs that weren't where they were supposed to be. They have compensated for uncooperative rainbows and steelhead. They have made my fly reel sing and fed me as I wandered through the wilderness of two continents. It's enough to make a guy wonder: Who the hell *was* Dolly Varden, anyway?

You have to love a gamefish whose name is derived from the imagination of another writer. In the case of the Dolly Varden, credit goes to none other than Charles Dickens, who describes the original version of his character by the same name in the 1841 novel *Barnaby Rudge:*

> *As to Dolly, there she was again, the very pink and pattern of good looks, in a smart little cherry-colored mantle, with a hood of the same drawn over her head and upon the top of that hood, a little straw hat trimmed with cherry-colored ribbons. . . .*

Barnaby Rudge was never one of Dickens's more popular works, and Dolly's name might not have made the long journey from London to the remote corners of the Pacific on its own power. Several decades after the novel's publication, however, someone resurrected the term in reference to a gaudy late-nineteenth-century style of women's dress that featured flowery prints and hats reminiscent of the fictional Dolly's garish taste in clothing. It was left to some inspired American frontier angler to imagine parallels between these outfits and the fish, thereby sparing us such uninspired alternative names as Pacific char.

I've certainly caught Dollies that evoked Dickens's original. One fall day in Alaska I was bowhunting grizzlies that were preying on spawning dog salmon along a small clearwater stream. The nature of this undertaking left little attention to squander. When the wind shifted and reappeared at the back of my neck, my bowhunt was over, and I sat down on a log to watch the fish.

Mature male dog salmon are extremely aggressive toward one another on their spawning redds. I was contemplating the nature of these biological impulses with grim fascination while a pair of twenty-pound dogs ripped into each other when I saw the first Dolly. A two-pound male, he was lurking slyly downstream of the redd, intent on a meal of dog-salmon caviar. It was not his behavior that caught my attention, however, but his appearance. The little spawning stream was gin clear—an unusual quality in the far north—and the fish glowed in the sunlight like a jeweled tiara, a riot of ruby and gold trimmed with exquisite white pectoral fins whose delicate outlines were plainly visible even from my perch well above the stream. The victorious male salmon eventually chased the intruding Dolly away from his turf, but my aesthetic imagination had been aroused. When I hiked back to the stream from camp that afternoon to set up my evening bowhunt, I came an hour early and brought my pack rod. Sight-casting to the voracious Dollies with single-egg patterns was almost too easy, but I didn't want to catch the fish so much as I wanted to look at them. Their colors were even more vivid close at hand, and I still think they may have been the most beautiful fish I have ever seen.

Those who first meet the Dolly Varden close to salt water or in an isolated alpine lake, however, may find such visual superlatives a bit strained. The fact is that few fish species demonstrate as much variation in appearance throughout their range as does the Dolly. Anadromous specimens are a virtually colorless silver when they arrive from the sea, while high-country Dollies may demonstrate only a pale reminder of the species' classic color scheme. That's how I remember the first Dolly Varden I ever caught: a drab three-pounder taken from an alpine lake outlet thirtysomething years ago. Of course I was just a kid then, and the fish was so chunky and substantial on the end of the fly line and again in the net that the washed-out quality of its pink and purple spots was of no concern whatsoever. It seemed like a beautiful fish to me, which is just as it should have been.

The difference between marine and inland versions of the Dolly is so striking that some authorities have argued that they are not even the same fish. This sort of taxonomic confusion is common in far-flung species successfully adapted to a wide range of habitat, and the Dolly is no exception. Western Montana bull trout were considered a subspecies of the Dolly Varden until recently, and even experts argue about the distinction between Dollies and arctic char. My own rule of thumb for telling these two look-alikes apart in the field is simple although perhaps not always foolproof. If the spots on the fish's sides are smaller than the pupil of its eye, the fish is a Dolly. If the spots are larger, you've caught yourself a char. And if you still can't tell the difference, rest assured that a whole lot of other people can't either, and that some biologists still argue that they are one and the same species anyway.

No one would dispute the fact that the Dolly can be a beautiful fish. It is its eating habits rather than its appearance that have gotten it into trouble over the years, for the sad fact is that the relationship between the Dolly Varden and sport anglers has a checkered past at best. The northern pike of the salmonids, Dollies prey upon almost anything, and a remarkable variety of birds, snakes, rodents, and whatnot have been recovered from their gullets by curious observers and amateur naturalists. They have a definite preference, however, for the young and vulnerable forms of trout and salmon, the more highly regarded species with which they share much of their range. In the bad old days of wildlife conservation, when management all too often meant inventing means and motives to kill species that seemed to be in the way, wholesale Dolly Varden eradication programs existed in several western states. Montana once offered bounties for Dolly Varden fins. Of course those Dollies were probably bull trout according to the modern classification, and bull trout are now a threatened species that the state of Montana is working hard to protect, all of which should tell us something about the fickle nature of wildlife politics. At any rate, the Dolly may be the only gamefish I have ever pursued that once carried a price on its head. As an outlaw of sorts myself, I find it easy to relate to this.

Even today, the Dolly is often dismissed as fare for bait and hardware anglers at best, when in fact the species has a lot to offer on the end of a fly line, where its voracious character finally emerges as an asset rather than a liability.

Dollies love salmon and steelhead eggs, as every enthusiast of salmon and steelhead knows, and single-egg patterns are good starting points, especially during cold water conditions in winter and spring. During summer months, downstream salmon smolt dominate the Dolly's menu in maritime drainages, and in the right place at the right time flashy streamers on #2 and #4 long-shank hooks can produce the sort of constant action that my friends and I stumbled into on that nameless Siberian stream. Even when feeding on other fish, Dollies tend to be methodical, so slow retrieves that keep the fly close to the bottom are usually most effective. When taken on streamers, Dollies have a stubborn tendency to strike at the very end of a quartering downstream cast, so it pays to let the line straighten completely and hesitate before retrieving.

And Dollies will rise to dry flies, although insects are a relatively unimportant part of their diet. I have taken them sporadically on hopper patterns and any of a number of large surface attractors. Dollies hardly qualify as selective trout, however, and the sight of them feeding on the surface should always be greeted with a certain skepticism. One spring day, I was surprised to see furious surface-feeding activity on a salmon stream I knew could hold nothing but Dollies at that time of year. The occasional lonely-looking mayfly coming off the water seemed an unlikely trigger for the feeding frenzy under way. Only after careful study did I realize that the fish were rising to old salmon eggs that were floating to the surface in the rising water. A well-greased single-egg pattern matched the "hatch" perfectly.

Let's be clear about one thing: On the end of a fly line, Dollies are not bonefish, or rainbows, or even brook trout. Overall, I would put their fighting qualities somewhere in the walleye pike–chum salmon class of freshwater gamefish, realizing that by doing so I have certainly offended some enthusiast of one of these species. Once again, there is a great deal of variation among individuals. I have hooked good-size Dollies that gave new meaning to the phrase "dead weight." Nod your way through encounters with enough of these characters and you'll be ready to join the cynics deriding the Dolly's sporting reputation. On the other hand, I have caught specimens that convinced me I had hooked a steelhead or silver salmon until I had the fish at bay. The bottom line? On light fly tackle, larger Dollies can be a lot of fun to catch. Enough said.

One other element of the Dolly's admittedly quirky appeal warrants mention, even though it smacks of the politically incorrect in these rigid times. Here it is anyway: Dolly Vardens taste good. This sort of statement produces immediate discomfort in catch-and-release circles, to which I myself belong in all biologically appropriate circumstances. Perhaps my regard for fried Dolly Varden simply reflects the fact that I have fished for them so often in wilderness circumstances when, in the course of hunting or exploring or whatever, what I caught was what I ate, and human consumption could not possibly impact such a vast untapped resource. Besides, Dollies really are fine table fare. Their rich flesh remains firm and inviting when cooked over an open fire; prepared in a real kitchen equipped with the tools of the culinary trade, it can become a gourmet delight. So while I'm certainly not advocating indiscriminate plunder of the Dolly Varden, I do suggest that if you kill and eat only one trout next season, do yourself, your table guests, and countless numbers of downstream steelhead a favor. Make it a Dolly.

Winding through a dense lowland forest of conifers and birch, the Kenai Peninsula's Anchor River is generally regarded as the northern limit of the steelhead's range in the New World. It isn't, but that's another story. When I lived on the Kenai, I visited the Anchor as often as I could during the brief window of autumn between the end of moose season and the arrival of the harsh northern winter, which is to say that I did not visit it often enough.

Perhaps because of these circumstances and my relatively casual attitude toward the Anchor, I never came close to mastering it, although I had friends who did. They knew where to go and what to do. I just went down and enjoyed the fall scenery and the Anchor's easy, accommodating pace; and on the rare occasions when the river offered me up a steelhead, the fish felt like some kind of reward for good behavior.

That kind of philosophical attitude served me well when the skies were clear and blue and the river tumbled along as easily as a favorite melody, but when the weather turned hard and ice started to claw at the edges of the stream, I sometimes needed more to sustain any kind of effort as I fished, even on the Anchor.

Today is just such a day. It happens so fast here in Alaska, this sudden slamming of the door on the previous season. Earlier in the week, when I decided to take this afternoon off to go fishing, the weather had been crisp but pleasant, still and invigorating. Now it is just plain awful: winds northwest at fifteen, ceiling indefinite, visibility one-quarter in freezing rain and snow. I could have stayed home, but today I wanted to fish the Anchor to get away, rather than because of anything the river itself had to offer, and outdoor adventures undertaken in this frame of mind seldom turn out quite the way they were meant to.

I am standing next to a long, even run where I once caught a steelhead. Everything about me is shades of gray, without a lick of color anywhere in the landscape. The wind has a genuine edge to it and I'm cold even before I set foot in the water. Fingerless gloves help, but there is still no life as we know it in my hands. It takes several minutes to get a fly tied on the end of the leader, and then there's nothing left to do but go fishing.

I do just that for an hour, which as hours go proves to be a fundamentally miserable one. The guides are icing, my fingers cannot grip the line, and there are no steelhead. Ordinarily the latter deficiency would not be much of a problem, steelhead being what they are, but today I am fishing under conditions that cry out for tangible rewards as well as philosophy.

Finally I pull up stakes and walk downstream toward the truck. I pass one last run before I climb up the bank and head for home, and it's the kind of water that looks too inviting to ignore, even on a day like this. The current is running smooth and even against the opposite bank and the flat, gray light makes the water look viscous, like syrup. It is just the place to hold a steelhead, and I know I won't sleep that night unless I drift the fly through it at least once.

I hurry back into the water before I can get a grip and change my mind. Even with the ice on the guides and the wind at my face the first cast feels like the one I came all this way to make, and when the strike comes I can imagine for an instant that none of the mistakes I have made in my life really matters anymore. After the initial shock of contact, the fish feels timid and insubstantial, and it's apparent at once that it's not a steelhead. After a momentary flash of disappointment, a wise inner voice advises me to relax and enjoy what the river has to offer. After all, it's a fish.

In fact, it's a Dolly some fifteen inches long, as colorless as the leaden sky. The fish sports that lean and hungry look, with a head one or two sizes larger than its body, and the fight it offers is anything but spectacular. But there it is, beached gently on the gravel bar, and despite its drab appearance and uninspired performance, one element of its presence there can never be taken away: The river has given me something for my trouble.

And so in the spirit of all this I unhook the fish and give it right back to the river, a decision that may be motivated by altruism or by the fact that it's just too cold to mess with a dead fish, no matter what kind it is or how it might taste. It doesn't matter really, not at this point, and I'm certainly too cold to worry about it further.

All I know as I hook the fly into the rod butt, reel in the last of the slack, and walk back up the bank on the first leg of the long journey home is that the Anchor River and I have come to an understanding of sorts, courtesy of the Dolly Varden.

From the wildest corner of the lower forty-eight states, north to Alaska, and finally east across the Bering Sea to the farthest reaches of the Pacific rim, the Dolly Varden has been cursed, kicked, and otherwise treated with all the misplaced animosity once reserved for wolves, raptors, and other misunderstood predators. It seems worth remembering that the Dolly's world is the lonely territory of fang and claw, the last of the planet's nontropical wilderness, where salmon are the vehicle that conveys protein from the sea to a hungry land and few rules of engagement apply among those who would harvest the bounty. This country is meant for its survivors, a fact that helps to put the Dolly's rapacious character in perspective.

No one today would argue rationally that the Dolly Varden should be gunned down in its tracks, as it once was. I merely suggest that we take this rapprochement one step further. Let's replace contempt with an ample measure of enthusiasm. Let's appreciate the Dolly's physical beauty and the romantic origins of its common name. Let's allow the Dolly Varden to save more of our days, and admire the rascals in our hands (and sometimes on our plates) when they do. We will all enjoy these fine wild places more as a consequence.

NINE

THE COLOR BROWN

Brown Trout: *Salmo trutta*

I CAN REMEMBER when you could stop at Yellowstone Park's Lewis Lake any time of day or night and enjoy your choice of campsites. Needless to say, this was quite some time ago. I still have fond memories of the Lewis Lake campground, memories that would be difficult to reproduce today: the marten that I treed there one afternoon; the cartoon-quality bears that strolled through the camp back when such goings-on were widely regarded as cute; the way the mist would hang above the polished surface of the lake early in the morning, before any adults were out and about to interfere with my own adventures. Above all else I remember Lewis Lake as the place where I caught my first trout on a fly.

I imagine that I was about five years old at the time. Somewhere in the unofficial family archives are collections of dated slides that would pinpoint my age, but the numbers aren't important enough to worry about. I remember that it was early in the morning, just before dawn, and the fog was so thick that my father and I seemed utterly alone out there in its midst, the only people on the lake if not the entire world. I remember the special quiet that comes nowhere except on still water just before sunrise, and how the lake pressed its chill right through the bottom of the canoe and into my legs as I knelt there. I remember the fly: a Woolly Worm, a pattern that passed for sophistication back in those days. And of course I remember the fishing, and the fish.

One thing about casting from a canoe in the middle of a still lake is that nearly everything beyond the gunwale is a legitimate target for the fly. This is an important consideration for five-year-old novice fly-fishers, and I'm sure its significance was not lost on my endlessly patient father. Every effort that resulted in the Woolly Worm's landing somewhere outside the canoe earned a quiet word of encouragement from the stern. As the sun rose behind us, the fog began to glow, and finally it no longer seemed possible to distinguish between the air and the water all around us. The fly would plop down out there somewhere and disappear, and I would twitch it back slowly as my father kept us gliding along as smooth and quiet as ghosts. Then came the seminal event of my early childhood. The line hesitated and then the rod came alive just for me. I remember my own cry of amazement. Behind me, my father offered the usual barrage of contradictory advice that experts shout at incompetent beginners in these situations (Give him line! Pick up the slack!). The trout simply did what trout have been doing since the days of Isaac Walton. Finally the leader appeared at the rod tip and the fish was there alongside the canoe. My father deftly slid the net into the water and the fish was mine. It did not seem possible that any experience could be more gratifying, and to tell the truth, I'm not sure I can remember one being so.

Oh yes, I remember that trout. It was my first on a fly, and it was a brown.

The dissemination of *Salmo trutta* from its home of origin in northern Europe to places like Lewis Lake (not to mention New Zealand and South Africa and Argentina) is a testimonial to three of the most remarkable forces in nature: the hardiness of the brown trout; man's ingenuity in the face of a problem truly worthy of solution; and the obsession of fly-fishers with the pursuit of their favored quarry.

Even in this era of technical marvels and vast resources, getting trout from places they are to places they aren't is no mean feat. (Actually this is usually just as well nowadays, but that's another story.) Imagine getting viable trout eggs from the British Isles to, say, Tasmania by sailing vessel in the days before modern refrigeration. Viewed purely as a technical challenge, the brown trout's diaspora must have been to wildlife biologists what manned space flight was to aeronautical engineers. But it happened, from one far-flung corner of the globe to another. No doubt about it; our fly-fishing ancestors loved their browns.

The brown trout's arrival here in the New World immediately influenced the development of American fly-fishing in two important ways, one biological and the other cultural.

By the late nineteenth century, agriculture had irrevocably changed the nature of trout habitat in the growing United States. The lower reaches of much of the country's free-flowing water was warmer and slower than it had been in its original state, which spelled trouble for native brookies in the East and cutthroats in the West. While it is true that the introduction of the brown cost these deserving species some ground, much of it was ground they were destined to lose anyway. In large part, the brown trout arrived just in time to fill one of those ecosystem vacuums that nature is known to abhor.

The new immigrants had a specific impact on the development of American fly-fishing, however, that went far beyond the simple fact that they were there to catch. Traditional Yankee fly-fishing methods focused on the brook trout, a lovely but not particularly cerebral species that required little from its pursuers other than that they be there. Visual masterpieces though they were, classical squaretail patterns were fished wet and did not resemble much of anything. The arrival of the shrewd, surface-feeding brown rendered obsolete this romantic but profoundly naïve approach to the science of fly-fishing. The need to deal with browns and their sophistication led directly to our development of the imitative dry fly and all the accoutrements necessary to fish it. One wonders, at times, how much simpler life would be if the brown had simply stayed on the other side of the Atlantic.

Yeah, but think what we'd be missing.

Among other things, we would be missing some world-class opportunities to be humiliated, which may not be a bad thing from time to time, at least at the streamside. When you *know* that you can catch as many fish as you want (yes, that actually happens sometimes, on bonefish flats and Pacific salmon streams among other places), the exercise eventually seems pointless. Of course one can argue that fishing when you *can't* catch fish seems fairly pointless as well. Then one might ask: Did you come here to fish or to argue?

Tonight, I have come to fish. It is almost nine o'clock and long evening shadows have finally coalesced into dusk. Nighthawks tear through the still air overhead and the sound of crickets rises from the darkness. This is my home water, and I know it as well as I know the design of my house, not that such knowledge guarantees anything when it comes to catching fish.

Here in the stream's lower reaches the trout population is evenly divided between browns and rainbows. Today, I have done the rainbows, thank you. A slow but steady hatch of #18 mayflies, scientific name unknown, came off this afternoon and the bows were in their feeding stations for nearly two hours, eager and basically brainless. They struck eagerly and they ran and jumped, and it was fun. Now, however, I am ready for something on a different order. I am ready to be challenged. In a word, I am ready for the browns.

The creek makes a right-angle bend at the head of this pool, gathering force as it swirls around the corner the way kids accelerate when they play crack-the-whip. The hydraulics have carved out a basin in the creekbed and the water there is deep enough to float your hat. When the resident fish feed, they do so in the eddy on the inside edge of the flow, lined up backward in the swirling current so that, viewed as part of the big picture, they are facing downstream. This means that presenting a fly reasonably requires accurate casts and complex mends. A stunted cottonwood tree leans out over the pool. I cannot believe that another season has passed without this tree falling victim to beavers or the law of gravity, but there it is, ready to eat as many dry flies as I care to feed it. In case you haven't yet put all this together into a composite picture, I'll draw the necessary conclusion for you. Fished in failing light like this, the pool is a bitch, a beautiful bitch perhaps, but still.

There are lovely little yellow stoneflies on the water. They have a scientific name of course, and I'm even reasonably sure that I know what it is, but for years I have gotten by calling these insects Little Yellow Stones, a practical name that serves my purposes just fine. The Little Yellow Stones are what scientists call an epiphenomenon, an event observed to coincide with another event, but without a causal relationship between the two. The presence of these distinctive insects is a reliable predictor of surface-feeding activity, a fact confirmed by the dimples in the eddy beneath the leaning cottonwood. But, Sophisticated Fly-Fisherman that I am, I know that the fish are rising not to the Little Yellow Stones but to #16 caddis emergers.

I tie on an appropriate pattern, take a measure of the drift, and roll the fly into a branch overhanging the head of the pool. The line snubs up, tight and unyielding. Now I can either wade through the eddy, soaking myself and spooking the entire pool, or I can snap the tippet and donate the fly to the brush. An easy choice, as it turns out; the function of the tying bench defined.

The tippet pops and the rebounding line runs halfway back down through the guides. My eyes are failing me. I turn downstream toward the fading sunset and run the leader back through the interminable series of wire loops. The tippet is history. Cursing softly but with no true anger, I struggle with a section of 7x, then another emerger. A memory surfaces like a feeding fish: my father, arms extended in failing light, wrestling with a tiny fly and cursing softly to himself. That may have been the first time I was aware of being able to do anything better than he could. The eyes go first, he said. He must have been about my current age at the time, and now I can see that he was right, even though I can't see much of anything else. All the while, the pool beneath the leaning cottonwood is coming to a slow boil, and I can hear more and more fish rising the whole time I'm struggling with the fly.

All right. Back in action at last, I false cast delicately between the treacherous willows lining the banks. Just enough light remains to reveal a dull suggestion of gold beneath each rise, confirming that the fish are indeed browns. I drop the fly, mend the line, and strike when a dimple appears at the spot where I think the fly must be.

Nothing.

The rise, of course, was meant for a nearby natural and not for my imitation. I can live with that. Lift, cast, mend. Strike.

Nothing.

Now let's get this straight. It's one thing to cast to an inert stretch of water and catch nothing, but it's another matter entirely to strike out in a section of water that looks like feeding time at the zoo. As a Sophisticated Fly-Fisherman, I resent such treatment. This is not sport, but rejection.

A dozen more futile presentations of the once reliable emerger point out the obvious: I'm fishing with the wrong fly. I substitute my own version of the Little Yellow Stone, knowing full well that it won't work, and it doesn't. The light is failing and I can no longer identify insects on the water save for a rough classification by size. The fish, of course, are going nuts right there in front of me, and the noise of each slurping take sounds like mockery in the darkness.

Desperation mounts; the meter is running. I can no longer tie on #18s, #16s, and finally #14s. The stream is too dark, the eyes of the hooks too small. I reach pathetically for my junk box, identify a Grayback by feel, and attach it to my shortened leader by the same method. Two casts later, the Grayback is in the tree.

Finally, it's too dark to fish. I retrieve the line, break down the rod, and slog back toward the bank. I can still hear fish rising out there in the darkness, even above the muscular gurgle of the creek.

Now tell me: Could any fish but a brown trout play tricks like that on a Sophisticated Fly-Fisherman like me?

Browns go through a series of transformations as they grow, and browns of different sizes can be very different things to the angler.

Small browns are naïve, eager feeders totally lacking in most of their elders' noble qualities. On my home water, we call eight-inch browns the Kiss of Death, for when they begin to feed, the chance of catching anything worthwhile all but disappears. Browns in the twelve- to sixteen-inch class are reliable, workaday gamefish more likely to entertain than to excite. At around eighteen inches, however, browns undergo a final transformation. These are fish with attitude, predators who depend less on drifting insects than on their ability to run down and devour other fish. They look the part, too: mean, heavy-jawed, and dark-spotted, with rich overtones of gold that often identify them the moment they flash behind a streamer. These are fish worth getting twitchy about. We call them *hogs,* and they are hogs in a way that no other fish with an adipose fin will ever quite approach.

Early in the season you can take them on the surface during the salmon-fly hatch, in which case you'll be sharing their favors with lots of company. You can float a stream like the Madison later in the year, pitch Muddlers into the pocket water along the bank, and hope to take a hog or two, which you probably will do if you stick with it long enough. You can take them on hopper patterns late in the summer on the right water and have yourself one hell of a time in the process. But my favorite way to catch hogs is to fish big, ugly nymphs in the spring when most people are thinking about other matters entirely. While something of an acquired taste and one that spring creek enthusiasts might never get around to acquiring, this style of fishing appeals to me for the most elementary of reasons: It works.

The Yellowstone River is an intimidating body of water even before spring runoff sets it clawing at its own banks. Broad-shouldered and powerful, the 'Stone is one of the few trout streams in Montana that looks as if it could reach out and grab you, which in fact it can. If you're accustomed to subtlety in the places where you fish for trout, this is the kind of water that can make you scratch your head and move on down the line to fish somewhere else.

That's just what I did for years, and I would probably still be driving right on by the 'Stone if my friend Dick didn't live next to it. His proximity to the river has made Dick come to terms with it the only way you can come to terms with one special piece of water, the one that you like to think of as your own. Since the Yellowstone no longer intimidates Dick, I can share a measure of his confidence when we fish it together, and that has given me a whole new outlook on a river that used to make my palms sweat.

The Yellowstone is giant stonefly water, and there are some things you need to know about giant stones. Forget all that business about the feeding frenzies salmon-fly duns supposedly induce on the surface. Other than providing calories for fish, their real contribution to the angling in a river like the Yellowstone is to concentrate large trout next to the banks where you can deal with them prior to the flies' emergence.

It is late May. I am rowing and Dick is casting. A couple of the kids are scampering around the drift boat, but I can't remember which ones. This isn't about kids anyway; it's about brown trout.

And about Big Uglies, the generic Montana name for all those weighted monster-size nymphs meant to imitate the underwater phase of giant stoneflies, the ones that come dressed in orange and black Halloween colors and carry enough lead to guarantee an audible plonk when they hit the water—or your head, in which case the plonk is likely to be followed by some choice expletives undeleted. There's nothing cute about Big Uglies. Whack yourself up alongside the head with one on a crosswind cast and you'll figure out how the Bitch Creek nymph got its name. At least that's my theory.

The water has started to rise and color up a bit as the year's first warm days push it toward the willows. The visibility is not a problem yet, although it may be by tomorrow. Dick is up in the bow of the drift boat, keeping the fly just alongside the bank as he casts, so close to land it's barely in the water at all. There are plenty of opportunities to hang up. Taking advantage of several of them, Dick has broken off twice in the first half mile of fishing. This is not a problem either. Big Uglies are easy to tie, and when you fish them, high water and break-offs are all just part of the territory.

Then the line hesitates again, but instead of meeting the bottom's dead weight, the rod tip pumps back enthusiastically. A golden flash appears down there in the dinge, a visual signature that can mean only one thing. This is not a whitefish or a rainbow. This is the genuine item. Let the year of the hog begin.

Managing a trout over twenty inches in a river as robust as the Yellowstone is a project. The line streaks through the current and then under the riverboat as I scramble to get oars and rods out of the way. The fish runs downstream and then back up again while I try to check us against the current. Minutes pass before Dick can begin to make any progress with the line, and then it's back and forth, give and take, past another hundred yards of water before it's time to call for the net. Finally the fish is panting alongside the boat, cradled gently in the net's mesh, as sullen in appearance as a trout can get. The fish's expression suggests that one of us owes it money. The jaw pouts and the crimson spots on its sides seem the size of dimes. One flick of the Bitch Creek nymph's shank and the fish is free to sulk its way back down to the bottom, to go right on being a brown trout until it's time to do this all over again for someone else.

Dick and I trade places. I work the line out overhead, mindful of the hook in the wind, and of the weight it carries packed beneath its chenille body like a blackjack. One of the kids is clamoring to fish. It's

Jenny, my own six-year-old. She is ready. Even at her tender age, Jenny has accompanied me through a good share of what the outdoors has to offer, and she has paid her dues in the process. I take her in my arms, brace her against the current's roll, and guide her through the first cast. I remember the trout we just released, and understand with sudden clarity why our ancestors packed clipper ships with tons of ice and nursed fish eggs all the way across the wild Atlantic just to bring browns to the brave new world that is now our own.

Jenny wants to do this herself and she won't take no for an answer. She lifts the rod tip and snaps it forward. Experienced heads on board duck as the Bitch whistles past above us. The fly hits the water with a plunk, just as advertised. Jenny giggles with excitement and then settles down to the business of fishing, even though she scarcely knows what that means.

I feel my daughter balanced loosely in my arms. What I feel is her intensity, the way she truly wants to catch a fish. Suddenly I can close my eyes and feel the chill of Lewis Lake pressed right into my legs again, and then it all becomes clear to me at last.

This is about kids after all.

TEN

THE PRINCE OF AUTUMN

Silver Salmon: *Oncorhynchus kisutch*

ALASKA PLACE NAMES are not always a reliable source of outdoor information. I've spent a lot of time on a certain Black Bear Creek without ever seeing one of the rascals, even when I was looking for them. I've never caught a halibut near Halibut Cove, and the last of the caribou were gone from the Caribou Hills long before I ever set eyes on them.

West Cook Inlet's Silver Salmon Creek, however, is a welcome exception to this list of ironies. There isn't much to Silver Salmon Creek, at least compared with most of the inlet's freshwater drainages, which tend to be powerful, foreboding glacial rivers that growl their way down out of the mountains toward the sea with little regard for whatever might lie in the way. You can cast a fly right across Silver Salmon Creek, and at low tide you can traverse its mouth in hip waders without worrying about keeping your feet dry. By Alaska standards, it's kid stuff.

The truly endearing quality of Silver Salmon Creek, however, is not its size but the clarity of its water. You *can* fly-fish glacial rivers, as our earlier encounter with king salmon demonstrated, but the experience is an acquired taste at best, requiring heavy gear, a willingness to battle cold, powerful water, and extreme faith in order to imagine something worth catching's being able to see even the largest streamers through all that murk. No wonder small, clear waters are held in such esteem by Alaska fly-fishers.

I still remember my first encounter with Silver Salmon Creek. On the flight across the inlet from my home that morning, Mount Augustine looked like a painting as it rose improbably from the sea, and beluga whales appeared as ghostly flecks of white on the inhospitable waters below. A commercial salmon-fishing period was open, so I flew the shoreline carefully looking for set nets, which have probably turned as many beach landings into disasters as wind and terrain combined. Finally I rattled to a stop and climbed out of the airplane, pleasantly alone.

I walked down the beach to the creek mouth and studied the first pool. The tide was falling, but the banks were still full. Silver salmon often reveal themselves in small water, but the pool was quiet, and I wondered if I might be a week too early. There was no way to resolve the question other than to assemble a fly rod and go exploring.

Finally my bulky streamer whistled through the air, plopped into the water against the opposite bank, and disappeared. The pool's tranquillity did not survive long. As the line tightened against the current's pull, the fly hesitated and I struck back. Suddenly a ten-pound silver was suspended in front of me at an improbable height above the water, utterly brilliant in the morning sunlight. No other gamefish I know jumps with such an unlikely combination of bulk and hang time.

Although a dedicated advocate of light tackle whenever appropriate, I don't mess around with fresh silvers. Even my heavy gear wasn't enough for that fish, however. After the first spectacular jump, it headed downstream with pure determination. Somewhere along the way it managed to wrap the leader around a rock, and we parted company. In the larger scale of things, our failed connection scarcely mattered. I had plenty of streamers and the creek had plenty of fish, most of them eager for the fly. Sometimes we stayed attached after the strike and sometimes we did not, and by the time the tide had fallen back down the beach there was nothing left to do but take a break and thank the sea for what it had provided.

Although it was a warm August morning, experienced Alaska hands will feel the yielding of the seasons at that time of year no matter what the weather. It is the time when the days seem to shorten before your very eyes, waterfowl begin to gather and to fly with purpose, and caribou shed their velvet. You can hear winter's footsteps bearing down on you then, and you draw the covers about you at night knowing that it's only a matter of time until you're overtaken.

But for the fly-fisher, autumn in the north holds a special appeal, for this is the season of the silver.

The definition of glamour fish is a potentially contentious topic, and one we shall explore in the contrapositive later on. Enveloped in mystique, these are the species that somehow wind up being more than the sum of their parts. Experienced anglers discuss them in hushed tones and travel long distances just to cast to water that suggests their presence. Everyone's short list of such species would include rainbows, bonefish, permit, and tarpon. Among anadromous salmonids, steelhead, Atlantic salmon, and kings come readily to mind. But if you were to poll a sample of experienced Alaska fly-fishers about the species that provides the most sheer excitement each season, the consensus selection likely would be none of the above. My money would be on the silver salmon, a relative sleeper by the standards of the heady company it keeps in Alaska's coastal rivers.

Although smaller than kings and less plentiful than reds, silvers are a riot on fly tackle. Just how much of a riot depends on where they're taken. All Pacific salmon begin to lose punch as soon as they enter fresh water to begin the upstream run to their spawning grounds. The rate at which this deterioration in sporting quality occurs varies considerably from species to species and even from run to run. Some early kings maintain their vigor for weeks after leaving the salt, while pinks sometimes seem to turn into cat food before one's eyes. While silvers generally fall well between these extremes, there is no doubt that a coho taken far from the salt water is usually just a shadow of its former self, at least on the end of a fly line.

All of which may explain why the silver salmon fails to make the conventional lists of glamour species despite its cult popularity among those who know it well. While silvers certainly can be taken on fly tackle in the open ocean, the needle-in-a-haystack aspect of their pursuit at sea makes them far better suited to means of take other than the fly. And while highly fishable numbers of silvers are often found concentrated in upstream holding water, they are seldom at their sporting best there. In fact, those who have the highest regard for silvers on fly tackle are usually those who have learned to fish for them where the best of both worlds meet: the complex estuarine environment of their home streams' lowest reaches, where the fish are bright and fresh and the tides promise a new set of rules and a new cast of characters every few hours.

While few would dispute that silvers from the tide line are silvers at their best, taking them consistently on a fly is always something of a challenge.

Determining where to fish is the first mystery to solve. While migrating schools of pinks, reds, and dogs are often obvious at a glance, silvers tend to travel in smaller numbers and favor deeper, out-of-the-way water where they are often hard to spot. In small, clear streams, however, even the relatively reclusive silver is sometimes quite visible. Walking high banks wearing good polarized glasses then becomes the best way to identify the water holding fish. In larger rivers and glacial streams, silvers are harder to locate unless they are active on the surface, as they sometimes are. But be advised that jumping, rolling silvers are not necessarily silvers interested in striking flies, an observation born of much frustrating personal experience.

The smaller the water, the more important tide and rainfall are to the salmon's final commitment to leave the sea. Under low-water conditions, silvers often stack up in the salt water off the river mouth, in which case that may be the only place to fish for them. In streams that cross wide beaches, fish seldom spend much time on the open beach itself. It's usually more productive to move upstream to the first deep run, where fish often hold after entering fresh water on a high tide.

In areas such as southeast Alaska, where small, clear streams and lots of silvers are the rule, typical creek-mouth terrain can both help and hinder the fly-fisher. Large tidal fluctuations and rocky creek mouths concentrate fish on falling tides and offer convenient rocks from which to work a fly line, but fish can be uncooperative on outgoing tides. Rising water, on the other hand, can make those handy casting platforms an adventure, and the angler who becomes too distracted by the fish may finish the day with a cold swim. Get yourself in the right spot at the right time, though, and the onslaught of motivated silvers can compensate for a lot of anxiety in the face of the incoming Pacific.

In larger rivers, of course, matters become still more complex. In contrast to other Pacific salmon, silvers do not feel obligated to keep their noses pointed into the current. They often seek out quiet eddies and backwaters, which may be difficult to identify at first. The definitive solution, of course, is that elusive factor known as local knowledge. In its absence, the savvy angler will look for structure that allows hard-working salmon a respite from the current's relentless assault. If the quarry is silver salmon, that is where the fish will most likely be. By happy coincidence, that is also the water that is easiest to fish with a fly.

Nowhere are these principles more apparent than they are on a river we have visited once already, the Kenai. While the Kenai's kings are definitive glamour fish, I didn't really mourn their passing every summer. I couldn't wait for late August, when those seventy-pound salmon and their attendant crowds and boat traffic would disappear, leaving local fanatics like me with quiet water full of cooperative silvers ready to take flies in the solitude of Alaska's ephemeral autumn. In the Kenai's lower reaches, the holding water is not always apparent at first glance. It took me several years to learn the silver holes, and even then the here-today–gone-tomorrow aspect of salmon behavior made a lot of running around by boat necessary to find fish consistently. All this sounds like a good argument in favor of a local guide for the visiting angler, and it is.

While I have great respect for those who take steelhead and even salmon on the surface, my own personal rule of fly-fishing for anadromous fish is that the fly should be near the bottom of the stream as much as possible. While sink-tip lines might seem an obvious choice, I use them for silvers only in large glacial rivers and the salt water itself. In smaller streams, I prefer the greater control that a floating line affords, and will accept in trade the need to get the fly down by other means. Needless to say, I weight almost all my silver flies on the tying bench, and use twist-on ribbon lead liberally to adjust the rate of sink to specific current conditions at the streamside.

While silvers can be spooky in low, clear water, leader shyness is seldom a problem near the tide line. This is no place for delicacy, so use as heavy a tippet as your line can handle. Even if you don't intend to keep the fish you catch, a stout leader will help the cause, since long, drawn-out fights add considerably to mortality after fish are released. For the sake of the fish, the catch-and-release angler should use enough tackle to get the job done right, and to get the fish back in the current and on its way upstream as expeditiously as possible.

A certain nihilism applies to the selection of flies for all salmon, grounded in the fact that no one really knows why the fish strike in the first place. While I have taken plenty of silvers inland on small flies and even single-egg patterns, I prefer junky streamers near the sea. To the best of my knowledge, it is impossible to use a fly too large for fresh silvers. Those who can't bring themselves to imagine using tarpon fly patterns on eight-pound fish should take a look at the tackle trollers use to catch those same fish in salt water. Silvers are by far the most naturally aggressive of the Pacific salmon species, and productive silver flies should be loud and large. The object is not so much to deceive as to attract attention.

It is early September. Mallards have started to organize into flocks and the bears are having trouble choosing between the berry patches and the salmon streams as they stuff themselves with calories in preparation for the winter. Ray and I are standing on opposite sides of a deep, clearwater stream's mouth on southeast Alaska's Prince of Wales Island. The tide is rising, and the confluence of the river's current and the incoming sea make it almost impossible to read the drift. The seaweed and limpets clinging to the rocks define the marine nature of the environment, as do the smell of the sea and the brilliance of the salmon jumping in front of us. It occurs to me that I cannot imagine a place I would rather be.

These are fresh silvers, the real thing by even the most rigid definition. Ray is a highly experienced fly-fisher who has taken his share of most of the world's major gamefish, the glamour species if you will. He has fished Alaska before and taken silvers on the fly, but never silvers like these, silvers so bright they flash unnaturally in the sun when they leap and justify every ounce of tackle you might bring to bear upon them.

There are plenty of fish visible this afternoon, but there is also plenty of water to contain them. Our fishing spot is less of a stream right now than a tongue of the ocean reaching in to lick its way around the rocks on which we stand. As the mix of fresh and salt water rises relentlessly toward us, we gear up, check our escape routes, climb onto a pair of strategically located rocks, and begin to cast.

Overhead, the sky is as clear as it gets in this country, and the light is doing strange things as it filters down through the conifers towering all around us. The shoreline is hidden in deep shadow for the most part, but the sun falls on the water in a brilliant mosaic of luminous windows through which the salmon leap periodically for reasons known only to them. When they appear, they are utterly brilliant in the isolated geometry of the sunlight; when they vanish, it's impossible to tell whether they have been claimed by the shadows or by the sea. They seem almost too beautiful to harness with instruments as mundane as hooks and lines. But not quite.

Ray is the visitor here. He should be the one to hit the first fish and he is. One minute he's stripping the streamer mindlessly through the complex weave of currents, and then his rod is right down in the water and nearly out of his hand. Taken by surprise, he fumbles with the drag and gets the rod up at last where its graphite spine can match itself against the fish. From my purchase across the way, I watch with satisfaction and remember Ray's skepticism during the hike downriver toward the sea. It seems unnecessary to say I told you so.

By the time Ray can pretend to have control over the situation, he has lost it. He's way down in his backing and the fish has taken him around one barnacle-encrusted rock after another. Six hours earlier, the scene of this battle was dry, but there's fifteen feet of cold Pacific there now, and that's more than enough water in which to lose a fish as motivated as this one. There's nothing left for Ray to do but hold on and hope, and hope can take you only so far in situations such as this. Suddenly, somewhere out in the marine debris, the line goes slack. Ray slowly reels in what remains, looking like a champ who has just lost a title bout to an unheralded challenger. To top it off, the tide has advanced so far that he'll go in up to his armpits as he scrambles back toward the latest definition of shore.

And to make matters worse, I will too.

When I lived in Alaska, I kept a long mental list of things that I missed about my former Montana home, but there was nothing I missed more passionately or persistently than fall. Autumn has always been my favorite season, the time when elk bugle and grouse flush and big brown trout appear by magic. Equivalent phenomena certainly take place up north, but fall in Alaska suffers from the same basic problem that afflicts frenzied adolescent lovemaking: It just doesn't last long enough. One day there are mosquitoes and tourists and more daylight hours than anyone can occupy outdoors and then it's winter, and nothing shuts down the show quite like the arrival of winter in Alaska.

Winter in that country is nothing to be trifled with. Going outdoors for the simplest purpose can evolve into an arctic survival exercise. It stays dark for weeks on end, people often drink too much, and the only fishing takes place through the ice, an activity whose appeal somehow eludes me no matter how desperate I am. It can be enough to drive a serious fly-fisher crazy, or back to Montana. In my case, I have friends who insist that it did both.

Perhaps it was that romantic longing for lost autumns that turned me into such a silver salmon enthusiast, even if the silver doesn't appear on most lists of fly-fishing's glamour species. Glamour, of course, exists in the eye of the beholder. Why people will endure shoulder-to-shoulder fishing for a chance at a king and then ignore their smaller but far more numerous and acrobatic cousins later in the season is beyond me. Not that I'm complaining, mind you, not with my regard for solitude.

So the silver salmon isn't a hot ticket in the public imagination. Fine. But trust me when I tell you that when taken at their best, silvers rank with the best. That means fishing for them when they're fresh from the sea, with tackle that will allow the fish to show what they have to show.

Taken on those terms, silver salmon have long served as a personal definition of the far northern autumn, itself a season of profound ambivalence. Like the bears, I often felt overwhelmed by the embarrassment of riches that confronted me then, especially since I knew what nature had in store just around the corner. One last bowhunt, one last flock of mallards circling the decoys, one last silver on the fly. . . . Up north, those are the true measures of the year's end no matter what the calendar says. It always fell to the silvers to make the most important promise: that we would all get through it somehow; that we would meet again next year.

And sure enough, we always did.

ELEVEN

WHITEFISH CAN'T JUMP

Rocky Mountain Whitefish: *Prosopium williamsoni*
(and friends)

I SAT DOWN THE OTHER DAY during a streamside lull and tried to come up with a life list of strange creatures I have caught on flies. Highlights included muskrats, bullfrogs, water snakes, a crested puffin, and a three-hundred-pound black bear. (Actually the bear broke me off on the first run, but that, as they say, is another story.) And this compendium didn't even include inanimate objects, the most memorable of which was what I can only describe as a sexual appliance that rose (if that is the right verb) to a nymph on my favorite local spring creek one evening, affording my fishing partners and me hours of fantastic speculation about its arrival. For months I considered running some sly ad in the lost and found section of the local paper, but I wasn't sure I wanted to handle the calls. In the end I settled for looking at everyone who lived upstream of that pool with a mixture of curiosity and respect.

It is indeed a jungle out there. No matter how focused one's efforts may be at streamside, incidentals always lie in wait between you and your intended quarry, whether brown trout or bonefish. These incidental catches can bring dismay, anger, and every once in a while a truly pleasant surprise. Some can earn you real respect playing "Guess what I caught this morning?" over dinner in camp, while others become such a nuisance that you just have to pack up and leave the stream. Every once in a while, one will manage to save the day. For better or worse, we all have to learn how to deal with them.

Consider, for example, the case of the Rocky Mountain whitefish, the most common such uninvited guest here in western trout country. The whitefish can't quite decide whether to call itself fish or foul. On the one hand, the state of Montana says in no uncertain terms that it is a game species, complete with limits and other legal trappings of privilege. And it does have an adipose fin, establishing its morphological relationship to trout and char. Unfortunately, it also has an adipose mouth, which, combined with its overall drab appearance and lackluster performance on even the lightest tackle, consigns the whitefish to the modified sucker category in the opinion of most trout enthusiasts.

Which would not be a problem, except for one curious element of the whitefish's lifestyle: In contrast to real suckers and other unequivocally low-rent characters with fins, its dietary preferences are very similar to those of the trout. When feeding on the surface, whitefish can usually be identified by their dimpled rise form, but that doesn't help much down deep, where they feed eagerly on the same caddis and stonefly nymphs that are so important to big western browns and rainbows. And so if you are nymph fishing almost any of Montana's premium trout streams, it will only be a matter of time until your line hesitates and you eagerly haul back to be greeted by the nearly dead weight of a whitefish. You may get fooled for a shake or two of the head, but the illusion seldom lasts long. I don't know if they really can't jump, but they almost never choose to, and they almost never do much of anything else worthwhile on the end of a fly line either.

Ray has a hard-and-fast rule to govern these situations: If you're catching whitefish, you're doing something wrong. Since they live in the same places and eat the same bugs that trout do, this principle may seem dogmatic, but he's adamant. Start catching whitefish and he'll insist that you change water, change flies, change something. Whitefish do seem to congregate in certain pools and riffles identifiable only through experience, and I'm hard-pressed to remember catching a lot of whitefish and a lot of trout in the same place at the same time doing the same thing.

Whitefish have their enthusiasts, of course. I have friends willing to spend long winter mornings waist-deep in frigid water just to catch them. Some of them claim that smoked whitefish tastes better than smoked salmon, but these are the same Montanans who will tell you that fried rattlesnake tastes better than fried halibut and lingcod tastes like lobster. One gathers that their judgment may not be the best in culinary matters, and perhaps in other matters as well. Their standard February reply to questions about their sanity is usually: "Well, what kind of fish did you catch this weekend?", and I suppose they have a point.

Way downstream from the usual blue-ribbon water, on the other hand, where the current starts to slow down and color up and the trout begin to cede their ecological dominance to warm-water species, another more interesting variation on the theme begins to appear: the goldeye.

Once again, credit the earliest description of the species to none other than Meriwether Lewis, who, on June 10, 1805, inspected a catch from the upper Missouri and noted that one component of the bounty "is precisely the form and about the size of the well-known fish called the hickory shad." Seventy years later, a young English butcher named Robert Firth settled in Manitoba, where he discovered that hot-smoking goldeyes from Lake Winnipeg turned this silvery scaled pan-fish from fertilizer to gourmet delight. Lake Winnipeg goldeye became a culinary staple throughout Canada, with British royalty and American presidents eventually counted among its enthusiasts. Fish stocks eventually declined, as they almost always seem to do when their dollar value exceeds a certain critical threshold of human greed, and the goldeye went the way of the buffalo tongue as a Great Plains staple.

But they are still there, for those willing to venture far enough off the beaten track to find them, which I usually do in the course of pursuing trout as far down the Missouri drainage as I can go and still pretend that I am trout fishing. Those willing to fish similar out-of-the-way waters will find two pleasant surprises when they finally encounter the goldeye, neither of which has anything to do with smoking and eating them: 1) They hit flies savagely, including dry flies. 2) They can jump, and they do so at every opportunity. Like little tarpon, actually.

I've never really understood why the goldeye hasn't attracted more attention as a gamefish. They're not large, of course, averaging a pound or so, but their aggressive character seems fair compensation for their lack of size. Lewis's original comparison of the goldeye to the shad still seems accurate, and anyone who can enjoy fishing for one ought to be able to enjoy fishing for the other. When it comes to introducing a kid to the pleasures of the fly, it's hard to beat goldeyes for cooperation. And if you're really motivated, you can fire up the smokehouse and re-create a classic gastronomic delight and a bit of Great Plains history all in one sitting.

Salmon streams have some incidentals of their own to serve the unwitting angler. One fine August morning I was prospecting for silvers near the mouth of a tiny creek on the west side of Alaska's Cook Inlet when something tagged my streamer near the bottom that didn't feel anything like a salmon. After a few dogged runs around the pool, I was able to hoist the fish into the shallows, where I discovered I had caught a flounder. I was faintly amazed, since I was several pools upstream from the sea and one does not ordinarily think of sole as fly-rod fare, even in salt water. Nonetheless, I caught several more from the same lie before I went elsewhere to look for silvers. And yes, everyone was impressed when it was my turn to play "Guess what I caught?" around the campfire that evening.

Salt water, of course, adds a whole new cast of characters to the story. Some years ago I seized upon the brilliant idea of catching a Christmas Island giant trevally by standing on the ocean reef on a falling tide and casting a tarpon fly into the surge between the coral and the blue water. This was a profoundly optimistic idea at best for a variety of reasons, not least of which has to do with the character of the giant trevally itself. The tenacity of the fish that took a hookless teaser plug a few pages back should have told me something about the chances of landing one in the surf, or even of returning with my fly line if I managed to hook one.

But no. So I swam out to the reef and struggled through the surge to the edge of the ocean itself and began to cast. The average length of time between the fly's arrival in the water and its disappearance into something's mouth was less than ten seconds. The somethings were a fascinating cross section of South Pacific reef fish weighing between one and three pounds. All fought like hell. Most broke my leader through some combination of teeth and sharp coral. I finally did hook a trevally, a dink in the fifteen-pound range, who treated me to the prompt and inevitable loss of my entire leader. As I slogged back toward the beach, my regrets were less for the loss of the trevally than for the leader, for now I could not spend the rest of the afternoon whanging away at reef fish.

Wading bonefish flats gives the interested observer an opportunity to look over all kinds of things besides bonefish. Some—barracuda and lemon sharks, for example—are well worth a shot if you happen to have at hand a rod rigged with a wire leader. Many of the most common varieties—rays and boxfish in the Caribbean, milk fish and parrot fish in the Pacific—hardly warrant a second look. That's what I always said about the colloquially named turbot, a dark, floppy-finned visitor to the Turneffe Island ocean flats that bears no resemblance at all to the Atlantic flatfish of the same name. Given the turbot's habit of fluttering along lazily on its side as it feeds, I couldn't imagine anything less inspiring to a fly-fisher until the day I actually hooked one. Its warp-speed retreat over the reef left me with a smoking reel, a new respect for turbot, and more than idle curiosity about the sporting potential of all those other odd-looking fish on the flats.

And the saltwater fly-fisher should never ignore the ubiquitous needlefish, bearing in mind what is in store should you land one. On one trip to the Bahamas, Sheli and I were drifting lazily off an empty flat when I saw a three-footer circling in the current. Because I was bored and there weren't any bones around anyway, I flipped my Nasty Charlie at the fish, which attacked the fly immediately. Lip-hooked, it couldn't get to the leader with its teeth, and it tail-walked around us in as fine a display of piscine acrobatics as I can remember. Finally it was time to get on with other things, so I reached down and grabbed the needlefish like a salami. Big mistake.

In retrospect, it was a profoundly stupid thing to do, an impulsive action that reflected more than anything the distance I live from the marine environment and its hazards. The needlefish tagged my forefinger like a pit bull. Attempting to release my finger by using the lever advantage of the fish's long beak simply led to involving my other hand in the disaster. Before we were done, the casting deck looked like the scene of a shark attack and the needlefish was retreating arrogantly toward deep water with my fly still embedded in its jaw.

Don't say I didn't warn you.

The purpose of this discussion is not so much to suggest serious fly-rod assaults on goldeye and turbot, but to remind us how arbitrary the distinction between gamefish and just-plain-fish fish can be. It's worth remembering how recently the bonefish fell into the latter category. The pioneering efforts of a few fly-rodders possessed with the vision thing elevated the bone from seagoing sucker to Cult Object within our lifetime. It is entirely reasonable to ask what overlooked species might be next.

During the last decade or so, fly-fishing has fallen victim to a regrettable sort of propriety. According to the new rules, it may be more important in certain circles to be able to say that one has gone to the Bahamas for bones or to Alaska for rainbows than to actually have a good time while you're there. And for victims of this mentality, it's difficult to admit that one actually enjoyed catching a species not (sniff) from the Approved List.

It's time to lighten up. Fly-fishing (or any other outdoor activity) should never become an excuse to lose one's sense of wonder at the natural world. From mountain streams to ocean flats, water is the source of most of the world's great mysteries, from wayward flounder to Loch Ness monsters. There should be some room in the curious fly-fishing heart for all of them.

It is March, and the high-plains winter has just started to loosen its grip on the country, the water, and our lives. I have driven down to Livingston for no other purpose than to get out of town. Those who don't understand this primal impulse cannot have spent three months as snowbound as the ones I've just endured. I am tired of feeling confined and it is time to travel, somewhere, anywhere.

Livingston is my standard destination under such circumstances, close enough to home to get to without a production, but far enough away to confer some anonymity and the freedom that implies. My friends Dick and Annie live there, right on the banks of the Yellowstone. Dick and I went to high school and medical school and served in the Indian Health Service together, and a friendship capable of surviving all of that probably doesn't have much to fear from anything.

Dick is still at work when I arrive, which is no surprise, since he's always taken that kind of thing more seriously than I do. His dedication inspires me, in fact, and I imagine that at some level my lack of dedication inspires him, which suggests just the sort of reciprocity good friendships should be about. As years go by, I find myself relying on Dick more and more to keep me abreast of the things I should be worrying about as a physician, while he relies on me more and more to drag him out of the office to do things in the outdoors. No problem; I'm good at that.

After a warm hello from Annie, I dump my gear next to the living-room couch where I always dump it and head outside toward the river, which as usual I view with a certain awe. The Yellowstone is just so much more *substantial* than my own home water. There are big trout there, and there are no doubt big trout right in front of Dick's house, and if I want to, I can even pretend that they're what I'm trying to catch.

In fact, the riffle in front of Dick's house is one of the premier stretches of whitefish water in the world. You can fish it right from his lawn without even bothering to put on waders, a wonderful convenience at times like this when you've just driven three hours over lonely roads and really want nothing more out of the day than the ability to avoid talking to people you don't want to talk to. Right now that seems just about my speed, but I can always remind myself that I'm fishing a Blue Ribbon Trout Stream if the need arises.

So here I am, wearing the same clothes I was wearing when I left my office hours earlier, plus a wool shirt to buffer the inevitable wind blowing straight down the pike from Paradise Valley. I've got my heavy nymph rod out with a George's Brown Stone on the end of the leader. The water has that sterile look that even the best trout water always has at this time of year, as if it were designed to preserve fish rather than to make them grow. That and the wind and the basically ridiculous nature of my attire make it hard to get too serious about any of this, but hey, I'm fishing, and damn near no one else is, including you.

I doubt that my friend George Anderson designed this fly to catch whitefish, but if he had, he could now lay claim to genius, at least among those who actually *want* to catch whitefish. It's a great Yellowstone trout fly, of course, and I can always pretend that's why I have one on the end of the leader, but I'm beyond that now. It has been a long, ugly winter and I want to catch a fish, any fish.

There is always awkwardness at the beginning of the year when casting skills have lain dormant over the winter like a turtle holed up in the mud. In the good years, I discover this principle on some bonefish flat in February when the fish are tailing right in front of me and I've got an acute case of fly-rod chaos in progress. This year I couldn't connive a warm-weather vacation to save my soul, and now my rustiness and the weighted nymph and the Paradise Valley wind add up to real trouble. Fortunately, there's nothing behind me but lawn and the neighbor's dog, who is something of a pain in the ass and not the kind of dog you would really mind sinking a weighted nymph into if it came to that.

Finally I have the nymph going where I want it to go, and I settle into the mindless process of trying to catch something with it. A curious intensity asserts itself as I follow each measure of the fly's drift through the riffle. I shouldn't care this much, but I do. The fact is that each little hesitation out there in the current could be the beginning of the first fish of the year, and you shouldn't have to make excuses for that.

Then deep in the cold current a fish actually takes (only a real optimist could call this a strike) and I've got myself a whole new outlook on the afternoon. If you want to read about fish running and jumping, you'll have to go on to another chapter, but that's not the point. That's a fish out there. It's on the end of my line. Contact has been made.

The Yellowstone holds some pretty good whitefish and this is one of them, the first of several, as it turns out. I land the fish, scramble awkwardly down toward the waterline in my civvies to flick the nymph from the corner of its fleshy mouth, and get right back to business. This may be the only day all year I actually enjoy catching whitefish, but that's the kind of thing you can always worry about later. Finally the temperature starts to drop and, although the guides aren't icing up yet, I know my tenure on the lawn is limited. These aren't steelhead, after all. Even fools sometimes recognize their limits.

Then I hear the sound of tires on gravel behind me. "What are you catching?" Dick's familiar voice inquires.

"Five-pound browns," I reply earnestly.

"Right," Dick says as he climbs from his car. "Looks like you need to come inside and thaw out a bit."

He's right, of course. I am poorly dressed for the occasion and the wind is getting to me. And yet as my shivering fingers secure the nymph in the rod's cork handle, I turn away from the water with a certain sense of regret. The river has treated me fairly. There are no grounds for complaint. A new season has begun.

TWELVE

GIFTS FROM THE SEA

Steelhead: *Oncorhynchus mykiss*

1. THE COUNTRY

A half-dozen old pickups occupy the parking lot outside the Black Bear Cafe. Their bumper stickers leave no doubt about the prevailing direction of the local ecopolitical winds: Jobs Not Wilderness; Timber Dollars Feed My Family. Inside, the argument becomes even more direct. Due to increasing government regulations, forest products are no longer available, reads a neatly lettered sign next to the toilet in the men's room. Wipe your ass with a spotted owl.

There you have it. This is logging country. In the mountains towering behind the Black Bear Cafe, great stands of mixed conifers—Douglas fir, western hemlock, red cedar, Sitka spruce—jut upward toward the lead-gray sky. The tiny communities that perch here between the mountains and the sea exist almost exclusively to harvest them. As one of the few remaining souls with room in the heart for both logging towns and endangered species, I always feel an acute sense of conflict when I step into a place like the Black Bear. Every so often I find myself asking the Rodney King question: "Can we all just get along?" The answer is usually no, and when my impulses to the contrary occur in loggers' hangouts like the Black Bear, the results of my attempts to suggest otherwise are inevitably disastrous.

And so today I walk quietly to a table intent on nothing more controversial than breakfast. Billed as a short stack, my order of pan-cakes arrives dripping enough butter, syrup, and cholesterol to choke a hog. No matter; this morning I've earned it. In the previous two hours, Ray and I hooked sixteen wild steelhead on flies. The morning became one of those rare conjunctions in outdoor sport when usually difficult matters become effortless, and in the end there was nothing left to do but express our thanks to the stream and walk away utterly sated.

Mornings like this make me wonder why Alaska's steelhead don't attract more attention among serious fly-fishing enthusiasts. In fact, there are reasons for this fishery's relative obscurity that are as obvious as the rugged terrain outside the grease-spattered windows of the Black Bear Cafe.

The northern limit of the steelhead's range is generally held to be the Anchor River on the southern end of the Kenai Peninsula. In fact, sev-eral small peninsula streams farther north support locally significant steelhead runs, and I have taken a large rainbow trout carrying sea lice from the tidal waters of one small stream on the west side of Cook Inlet, of which fact you may make what you wish. Nonetheless, the heart and soul of Alaska steelhead fishing is to be found in the state's southeastern panhandle.

A brooding stab of land wedged between Canada and the North Pacific—Southeast, as the region is known to Alaskans—has the privi-lege of supporting our planet's largest temperate rain forest. The dis-tinction between a temperate rain forest and its more familiar tropical cousins is that instead of being warm and wet, the weather is cold and wet. Rainfall in the heart of Southeast's steelhead country sometimes exceeds two hundred inches per year, and that is one hell of a lot of rain. Fishing often takes place in tidally influenced water, and South-east's twenty-foot tides can make trails and river crossings appear and disappear every few hours as if by magic. To add to the obstacle-course qualities of the terrain, the undergrowth that sprouts along these water-courses brings new meaning to the concept of impenetrable brush, and if it weren't for the bear trails along the streams, the banks would often be impassable.

The streams themselves are short and steep, quick to go out after a rain and quick to come back into shape again. Some are called rivers, but that is generally verbal inflation. These are small waters. Only a few—the Situk, the Karta, the Naha—are known at all outside Alaska, and even these have limited followings. You have never heard of my own favorites, some of which don't even have names on the USGS topo maps that are essential to a true exploration of the area. They are reached by boat or float plane or ambitious hike, and getting there, as they say, is half the fun.

In short, this is not easy fishing. A quick review of my Southeast Alaska steelhead survival kit helps put matters in perspective: raincoat, rain pants, rain hat, ankle-fit hip waders, leather gloves to keep the dev-il's club out of my hands, tweezers to remove the thorns when they get there anyway, tide table, plastic bags full of dry socks and matches, and a space blanket in case I have to spend the night in the woods, which I do about once a season. Oh yes: If bears bother you, bring along whatever it takes to make you feel comfortable in their presence, for you will certainly see their sign even if you are not fortunate enough to see the bears themselves. I personally recommend nothing other than common sense and a light heart.

With all this standing between the fly-fisher and the fish, it seems worth wondering why one would bother at all. Back inside the Black Bear, the waitress is standing by with a fresh pot of coffee. A cheery transplant from the British Isles, she is intent on telling me the story of her life as an Alaskan. At the next table, eggs and smokeless tobacco are being consumed with hearty enthusiasm, while I have scarcely breached the perimeter of my own breakfast. This seems an opportune time to settle back with another cup of coffee, collect my appetite, and explore the steelhead's mystique.

2. THE QUARRY

The fly, a Green Butt Skunk, plopped easily into the smooth reaches of the current and disappeared beneath the water, which looked like smoke after the previous evening's rain. This was one of many casts that morning, and I had settled into the rhythm of presentation as eas-ily as if I were practicing some kind of dance. So far, there had been no interruptions from the fish. This time the fly hesitated as soon as it found the smooth layer of flow just above the stream's gravel bottom. For those who squandered as much of their youth at this sort of thing as I did, no more formal announcement is required. When I hauled back on the line and raised the rod tip and the stream finally came to life in my hands after all those hours of silence, I felt as if an old girlfriend had just blown me a kiss.

The fish roared upstream through the riffle at the head of the pool without hesitating. Fortunately, this hookup took place in one of the stream's few runs that was not choked with downed logs, and I could see nearly a hundred yards of clear water above me. The fish consumed a good part of that distance as easily as an Olympic sprinter. For a moment it looked as if it was headed on up into the next pool, and I began to worry less about landing the fish than about saving my only fly line.

Suddenly and inexplicably, the steelhead turned, and my hand ground furiously at the reel as I struggled to recover the sharp coils of backing left behind. When the fish sailed past me toward the sea, a sixty-foot belly of line hissed through the water in its wake, just looking for some obstruction on which to foul itself. Because the fish chose to spend the next ten minutes running up and down the stream instead of just up or just down, and because the water happened to be free of debris and I had hooked my quarry solidly in the jaw, I eventually managed to bring it to bay in the shallows against all expectation. Finally, I reached down and slipped the bedraggled fly from its mouth with a hemostat. Bearing just the faintest blush of pink along its sides, the steelhead suggested an odd marriage of gentility and power. It seemed so unrepentant in defeat that I did not even try to position it in the water for a photograph. I could not imagine a camera doing justice to a fish like that one, and now as I remember the morning and try to get the feel of the encounter down just right, I still can't. To make matters worse, I'm not sure that a typewriter is capable of anything better.

Which is why, in short, normally sane people do all the things they have to do in order to fish for steelhead in Alaska. Simply stated, no one else can ever do it for you. Since you cannot rely on rascal writers or photographers, you're just going to have to take a look for yourself if you want to see what all the fuss is about.

Steelhead come shrouded in an aura of mystery. After countless hours spent addressing cold and heartless streams, some people simply refuse to believe that steelhead exist. For them, there is nothing to be

---

done. Even those who do believe in steelhead have to acknowledge a certain ambivalence about the object of their belief. For years, biologists argued whether these great fish were salmon, which they resemble functionally, or rainbows, which they resemble in appearance as well as in the public imagination. It turns out that everyone was right, as we saw earlier in this book. This news was a great relief to everyone except those who still could not catch them, and who consequently did not care what kind of fish the steelhead turned out to be.

Alaska steelhead are often said to run on the small side and this is generally true, as long as you regard eight- to ten-pound fish as being on the small side of anything. But it's worth remembering that the largest sport-caught steelhead in the world was taken near Ketchikan, right in the heart of my favorite steelhead country. Granted, this specimen was taken in salt water, which makes it not quite a steelhead by fly-fishing standards, but the fish was obviously going to run upstream somewhere. This specimen weighed forty-two pounds. It is difficult to imagine just how big a forty-two-pound steelhead really is. Years ago in Washington State, I remember a sometime fishing companion taking a two-steelhead limit, with each fish weighing over thirty pounds. That was in the Bad Old Days when people still whacked every steelhead they caught, and I still vividly remember the sight of that awesome brace of dead fish, albeit with a note of sadness. At any rate, even those of us fortunate enough to know what thirty-pound steelhead look like have trouble imagining forty-pounders. The mere thought of sinking a fly into such a fish is enough to cause sleepless nights for an entire season.

And they are out there.

3. THE PURSUIT

Because Alaska steelhead streams are small and clear, sight-casting is often possible, which is something of a mixed blessing. The opportunity to spot fish certainly increases efficiency, and the potential for excitement that sight-casting creates needs no explanation to veterans of spring creeks and bonefish flats. Steelhead do spend a lot of time in uncooperative moods, however, and it's depressing to discover how many times one can ignore a perfectly presented fly. Further, the most visible fish are often spawning, and I just don't feel right about fishing to spawning steelhead, no matter what they say in Michigan.

As much as the next fisherman, I enjoy tying elegant flies whose lineage obviously derives from classical Atlantic salmon patterns. The reality of Alaska steelheading is that, under most conditions, anything above and beyond single-egg patterns is usually window dressing. This cynical view is grounded in experience. So fire away with your Speys and Comets and Skykomish Sunrises, but when you've donated two hours' output from the tying bench to the bottom of some nameless, snag-filled creek in a matter of minutes, remember (if you wish) that a puff of orange yarn tied around a hook would probably catch just as many fish.

In terms of fishing technique, I am proud to report that I have not one original thought to offer, which confirms that I spend my stream time fishing like a maniac rather than trying to be thoughtful. I do cling stubbornly to the belief that, to catch anadromous fish on a fly, one should fish close to the bottom. There are purists who live to dispute this principle, and I admire them. I also reserve the right to fish my methods of choice within certain broad limits of decency, and so I will go right on dead-drifting unimaginative flies along the bottom simply because it feels like the right thing to do. It also works. The steelhead is one species whose pursuit demands no frills, since the fish itself can provide all the intrigue one could ever ask of a trout stream.

I fish floating lines almost exclusively because they allow better control than do sink-tips, they obviate the need for strike indicators (which I dislike), and they are more fun, which should require no explanation. Leaders should be kept short and light for approximately the same reasons. I do not, however, use light rods, because when I hook a fish I want to land it or break it off in short order. Long, tentative battles are hard on steelhead. An Indian friend from central Alaska once expressed to me his dismay at the entire concept of sportfishing. Playing with food, he called it, and he had a point. I reserve the right to play, but there is no reason to drag the process out beyond the boundaries of good taste.

In the end, there is little that is glamorous about fishing for Alaska steelhead other than the fish. This is not the place for long, graceful double-hauls and arcane discussions of tackle. The fish themselves are the story's major characters, and that is as it should be.

---

4. STEELHEAD BOB

I first saw Steelhead Bob (I know nothing more of his name) on a small, remote stream where I really had not expected to see anyone. This sort of thing happens in Alaska more often than one might expect. I just stumbled through the last of the underbrush one day and there he was in the next pool below me. It seemed silly to jump out and announce my presence, so I sat down on a log and watched him fish his way up the stream toward me, without really meaning to be sneaky.

While he was obviously fly-fishing for steelhead, he was going about it in his own way. As I watched, he attacked the fast water with short, staccato casts that barely let the current touch the fly. When he finally came close enough so that I could see what was on the end of his line, I received another surprise. A huge concoction of feathers and hair occupied the end of his leader as if by accident. Had I rummaged through all the old tackle boxes in my garage, I would have been hard-pressed to find anything that seemed less likely to catch steelhead, with the possible exception of the tube lures that I sometimes let the kids peg across the flats at barracuda. I might have dismissed him as just another guy who didn't know what he was doing except for one disquieting fact: During his progress through the pool, he hooked and landed two fish and I hadn't touched one all afternoon.

I wound up talking to Steelhead Bob for some time, and the conversation, as one might imagine, centered on steelhead. While he has vague geographic attachments throughout the Pacific Northwest, he cheerfully describes himself as homeless, which really means that he is free to follow the fish. Equipped with boat and camper, he lives the mobile, focused life of a steelhead commando. As nearly as I could tell, he has fished every steelhead stream I have ever heard of and forgotten more about most of them than I will ever know.

What finally impressed me about Steelhead Bob, however, was not the way he caught steelhead but the way he cared about them and allowed them to reign over his life. It's difficult for the uninitiated to imagine any fish inspiring such devotion, but it happens. Bonefish do it; so do marlin, Atlantic salmon, and brown trout. But when it comes to making people cross that indistinct line between enthusiasm and obsession, none gets the job done quite like the steelhead. Perhaps this is partly a function of the whole miraculous business of their return after so many long miles at sea. Every strike seems like the fulfillment of a promise. Certainly, if I were going to take a year out of my life to pursue one species of fish exclusively, my quarry would be steelhead. They do that to you; just ask Steelhead Bob.

If you can find him.

5. THE FUTURE

The bridge gave me elevation, which helped, but the angle of the light wasn't right and I had to squint uncomfortably through my polarized glasses as I looked for fish. A slick spot in the current below formed and dispersed with tantalizing irregularity, revealing a light-colored gravel bottom upon which there sometimes was and sometimes was not a dark shape like a steelhead. Because I was concentrating so intently on the search for fish, I didn't see him approach, and I thought I was alone until I heard the crunch of boots in the gravel beside me. "Good morning," he suddenly announced with an easy smile and the earnest intensity of a missionary. "I'd like to talk to you for a minute about releasing wild steelhead."

I assured him at once that this was one of my favorite subjects, that I did not believe in killing such fish, and that, in short, he was preaching to the choir. No matter; my visitor had things that he needed to say and he said them with a quiet eloquence born of conviction. While I ordinarily have a limited tolerance for other people's opinions, especially when they're delivered without invitation, the subject was so worthwhile and the speaker so sincere that I found the listening easy. Finally, we shook hands and he disappeared into the brush along the stream. As I turned my attention back to the possible fish in the run above the bridge, I could not help but feel that the stream and the world it flows through are better places because of such people. That isn't a feeling I experience often.

Even in the best of times, it isn't easy being a steelhead. The species faces intense predation at every stage of its complex life cycle, from egg-gobbling Dolly Vardens on the redds to hungry marine mammals at sea. They are especially vulnerable in their spawning streams, where lack of rain or an ill-timed flood can threaten an entire generation of fish. To this list of natural heartaches comes the hand of man, bearing freshwater habitat degradation due to injudicious logging practices, marine oil spills, and, most critically, high-seas interception by "squid" fishermen.

Faced with this litany of hazards, it's sometimes hard to imagine that a few people armed with fly rods can have any impact on steelhead runs. From such a perspective, catch-and-release seems more a matter of style than biological principle. One must remember, however, just how small Alaska's wild steelhead runs really are. The largest rivers may host five hundred returning fish each year. Most of the streams I fish support far fewer. In such waters, a few good rods in the right place at the right time can hook a fair percentage of a year's return in a day or two. This is an awesome responsibility, not to be taken lightly.

Back outside the Black Bear, the day is shaping up as another chapter in the saga of Man Against the Tongass. Groaning beneath the weight of felled trees whose diameter exceeds my height, logging trucks hurtle down the road, indifferent to whatever might be coming in the opposite direction. I have never driven a vehicle substantial enough to provide any argument.

This is a hard land at best, and it almost seems too much to expect a species as biologically vulnerable as the steelhead to endure here. Farther south, man has addressed the inevitable conflict between his selfish interests and the fish by building hatcheries and trying to replace the wild runs with what comes out of them. Unfortunately, once you've known the real thing, catching hatchery steelhead becomes the sporting equivalent of dancing with your sister. When you start accepting hatchery-produced zombies as an acceptable substitute for wild steelhead, you have essentially conceded the battle.

A light rain has started to fall, settling the dust kicked up by the logging trucks. I have made my peace with breakfast and the waitress, who still seems delightfully awe-struck by the fact that she is in Alaska rather than London, even though she's evidently been here for years. The rain offers hope for fresh fish on the next tide, and hope, ultimately, is what provides the foundation for the steelhead mystique.

I happen to have just the place in mind to search for them.

THIRTEEN

JUST ONE FISH

Arctic Grayling: *Thymallus arcticus*

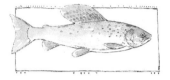

I WAS NUMB WITH FATIGUE, and I didn't have another grizzly bear left in me.

We had scrambled out of the Soviet military helicopter to discover that the salmon run had been and gone, and when it went, the bears we were searching for had evidently gone right along with it. Unfortunately, by the time we made this discovery the helicopter was airborne, so there we were alone in the Russian wilderness with our bows and our survival gear and no fish and no bears.

At first there was nothing to do but let the foolish feeling sink in as the extent of our miscalculation became apparent. Then we all sat down on the gravel bar and boiled some water for tea. By the time the kettle was hot, we had finished bitching in all the various languages at our disposal and gotten down to the business of reviewing our options. There was another salmon run headed toward us somewhere downstream from our position, and after a tense strategy session we decided there was nothing to do but march to the sea like lemmings and hope that we found the fish and the bears that would be feeding on them. The things one will do in order to take a grizzly bear with a bow and arrow.

That had been three days and fifty hard miles ago, which explains my state of exhaustion. I didn't have another grizzly in me because I had been within twenty yards of large bears twice that day without

108

getting a shot and I was out of adrenaline, an adequate supply of which is an absolute prerequisite for such a fundamentally ill-advised undertaking.

So as we made camp on the third day, I decided to leave my longbow behind and go fishing. One of the great delights of wilderness exploration is the sense of anticipation that comes from addressing unknown water with a fly. We had been so busy with bears that the river and its contents were still something of a mystery. The water was certainly beautiful enough, and it looked like one long, liquid invitation as it tumbled its way downstream toward the North Pacific.

We knew that our river contained pink salmon because the sandbars were ankle-deep in their carcasses and the air felt heavy with the odor of their decay. Overripe humpies may be a hungry grizzly's delight, but they aren't good for much on the end of a fly line. I really wanted to catch some of the big anadromous Dollies that seemed so plentiful in most of the region's drainages. This wish was based on both the excellent fighting qualities of these vigorous char and the fact that we were nearly out of food. I even entertained the possibility of finding *kundzha,* an exotic, tackle-busting species we had encountered earlier in other nearby rivers, and of which we shall hear more later. To be perfectly honest, I didn't really care what was out there as long as the weather stayed beautiful and I didn't have to stalk within bow range of another grizzly for a while.

Once we had the tents up and our basic camp chores completed, I took my pack rod and belly bag and followed the bear tracks upriver to a likely-looking run. There I sat down on a log, watched the river go by, and reviewed the day's events. But before I could lose myself too completely in the analysis of those close encounters, the unmistakable dimple of a feeding fish appeared on the surface of the clear water, making me an idle spectator no longer.

In the Far North, surface rises often arouse excitement in the flyfisher's heart out of proportion to their significance. Despite the sometimes staggering volume of fish in these cold waters, there is a certain sameness to most of them and to their taking that after a while begins to numb the imagination. Despite what biologists (and writers) have to say about the unique flavor of their individual qualities, most of these fish are basically big, silver salmonids that strike gaudy streamers aggressively and don't think much about anything while doing so. Fish feeding on the surface, however, suggest an entirely new set of possibilities.

I dug out my polarized glasses and began to pay more attention to the water. A good number of fish were rising out in the current, although I could not tell just what kind of fish they might be. An unfamiliar mayfly was emerging sporadically. It was large and gray, and I didn't know anything more about it except that the fish seemed to be eating it. Since angling was not the primary purpose of our trip and weight had been important when we packed, I had nothing but my skeleton wilderness tackle with me. From beneath the layers of battered streamers and egg patterns I did manage to find a few dry flies, each of which dwarfed the natural out on the water. Somehow, I sensed it wouldn't matter, and it didn't.

I tied on a moth-eaten Goofus Bug or some graceless equivalent and climbed up onto a rock at the edge of the water. This was no time to worry about delicacy of presentation, and when I finally let the line fly through the guides, the Bug hit the surface like a plane wreck. From my elevated position, I could see a dark-green shape detach itself from the rocky bottom as the fly drifted overhead. The fly and the shape converged lazily until a widening circle appeared around the Goofus Bug's bulky outline. I struck and missed, and the shape descended and disappeared into the crystalline reaches of the current.

I made a hard false cast to shake the water from the fly's hairy wings and laid the line out again. The shape (or one just like it; it's hard to tell about dark-green shapes) reappeared on another intercept course, and this time when the strike came I did nothing until I felt something on the end of the line. When I struck this time, the fish was mine.

I have searched the empty corners of my imagination for ways to make a grayling's fight sound challenging and I just can't do it. Rather than get lost in a lot of empty flourishes, I'll simply tell you what happened next. The fish shook its head a few times, played dead, and I hauled it to shore. There you have it.

Fortunately, the sporting value of the arctic grayling does not depend on runs and jumps. If that is where your vicarious needs lie just now, you are well advised to go on to another chapter. The grayling is neither an athlete nor an intellectual giant, but there are still two absolutely wonderful things about it: The first is the grayling's lighthearted approach to whatever you happen to have on the end of your leader. This naïveté guarantees that you can enjoy its company even when you're not in the mood for fly-fishing's technical demands, which is often the case in grayling country. The second is the aesthetic surprise when you finally get one in your hands, as my Russian representative of the species illustrated so well.

The dorsal fin is the grayling's obvious attention-grabbing feature, and one that certainly warrants a careful look. Immense and graceful, in full display it suggests something out of a fairy tale. Nature doesn't make things just because they're pretty (I guess), and as is usually the case with exaggerated appendages, this one's function includes threat, as my Siberian specimen demonstrated by extending and retracting its own dorsal fin for my benefit. In the process, the fish identified itself as a male by the way the fin widened toward its caudal half.

The grayling's marvelous colors are subtle but equally compelling to the careful observer. It is the freshwater counterpart of the dolphin; no other gamefish manages quite the same magic with its hues. As I rotated mine a few degrees back and forth in the low northern sunlight, it turned from gray to green to gold until its scales finally gave off a sort of lilac glow that occurs nowhere else in nature.

Finally it was time to get this one back into the water before the magic was gone forever. I wanted to catch a few more just for the hell of it, as a consequence, I suppose, of the urge to see what this new water really contained and to feel how its fish might behave on the end of a fly line. I would have enjoyed catching some char in addition to the grayling, to fight and to carry back to the waiting skillet. Rested and refreshed already by my encounter with the river, I even found myself wondering against all odds about walking back to camp, stringing my bow, and setting off to see if I had another grizzly left in me after all.

It is amazing how catching just one fish on a dry fly can affect the rest of the day.

I know that this collection is supposed to deal with fishing rather than hunting—with grayling, in this case, rather than grizzly bears—but the fact is that *Thymallus arcticus* and *Ursus arctos* share more than similar last names. Their native ranges overlap quite precisely and with little regard for traditional distinctions between the Old World and the New. It is as if both species had been poured like paint from a bucket over the top of the world and left to dribble down from the north until they ran out of momentum.

On this continent, both grayling and grizzlies still enjoy population strongholds in wilderness Canada and Alaska, while suffering from incompatibility with man along the southern perimeters of their range. Despite the amount of time I have spent enjoying both species in the Far North, Montana grizzlies and Montana grayling still hold a special place in my heart, for this is where I first met each of them years ago. That first encounter with the grizzly is, as they say, another story, better suited for another time. My first grayling, on the other hand, is worth remembering right now.

That introduction took place on the North Fork of the Big Hole River during the 1950s. At the time, the North Fork was a pristine little stream connected to its brawny, famous big brother only by its name and the law of gravity. I was a kid then, and the North Fork was just my size. It contained plenty of small, none-too-bright trout, a description that applied to me as well. There never seemed to be anyone else on the North Fork, and the fishing there was as easy and uncomplicated as fishing is likely to get.

During one of my family's periodic outings on the North Fork, we set up camp one evening, and after the usual warning about snakes, my parents turned me loose to work my way up through the open meadows above our tents with my fly rod, an indestructible length of fiberglass that somehow survived an entire childhood squandered on the backwaters of America. I was fishing a bulky dry fly that would now be known euphemistically as an attractor, which is just a dignified way of admitting that we don't know why Royal Wulffs catch fish, but I knew with all the certainty of youth that I was casting the best of all possible flies onto the best of all possible trout streams.

Somewhere in the course of the first riffle, my Royal Whatever disappeared into a dimple on the surface, and something felt out of place at once. The energetic resistance of even a small trout on a fly rod felt muted; I thought I might have hooked a whitefish or something even less prestigious. After a little head shaking and sulking beneath an undercut bank, the fish was in my hand, where its magical colors and sail-like dorsal fin confirmed at once that I had taken something special. I kept the fish, because it had yet to occur to most of us to do otherwise, and back in camp my father identified it as a grayling. I remember staring at my prize for a long time as the twilight faded that night, and the look of the fish got all wrapped up with the fine, lonely feel of the meadow—the grayling's vulnerable beauty and the wildness of the place somehow part of the same phenomenon. In that conclusion I was, with the uncanny prescience of youth, quite right.

The Big Hole drainage's population of native grayling now stands on the brink of extinction for all of the usual reasons, which should come as no surprise. Grayling, like grizzlies, coexist uneasily with human beings and inevitably come out second best in the conflicts that arise between us. Northern Michigan, for example, was once home to a unique grayling species (*Thymallus tricolor*) that enjoyed the dubious distinction of being the first American gamefish biologically annihilated by outdoor writers, who hyped the poor Michigan grayling so mercilessly toward the end of the last century that it was literally fished to death within a decade of its discovery by the popular sporting press. Lured by visions of its bounty, visiting anglers swarmed to the fish's haunts by the trainload and left wheelbarrows full of grayling carcasses to rot in the sun. At least the Michigan community of Crawford had the class to change its name to Grayling in honor of the fish that had been and gone in the waters nearby, which is how the grayling earned the distinction of being one of only four gamefish examined in this collection to have a real American town named after it. (Quickly, trivia fans, can you name the other three?) I suppose that's better than nothing.

The fact is, the grayling is a naïve country cousin with little ability to withstand anything remotely resembling fishing pressure. Coupled with its fastidious requirement for cold, clear water, the grayling might seem doomed to the same fate as another beautiful loser examined earlier, the cutthroat. The grayling does have one biological attribute in its favor, however: a huge reservoir of as-of-yet unassailable wilderness habitat in the Far North that extends across the top of two continents. Pessimistic as I am about the prospects for survival of vulnerable wild species, I would suggest that even this vast ecological security blanket not become the basis for complacency about the future of the grayling.

What of the grayling on the end of a fly rod? In two words: kid stuff. While widely regarded as one of the few true insectivorous gamefish in the Far North, from the fly-fisher's perspective grayling seem universally ready to eat almost anything, and they turn out to be more opportunistic and less genteel than their appearance suggests. In addition to the usual attractor-style dry flies and nymphs, I have caught grayling right and left on egg patterns and have had them vigorously attack large streamers meant for salmon and rainbows. The limiting factor in the selection of flies for grayling is not style or presentation but the size of the hook in relation to the fish's tiny mouth, a problem first commented on in print by none other than Izaak Walton a long time ago indeed. After a few days of fishing for silvers or rainbows with weighted flies, however, I'm often ready for some variety on the surface no matter what the trade-off in size and temperament on the part of the fish. Nothing in the north is more likely to provide it than the grayling.

In arctic habitat, where fly-fishing often becomes a matter of pitching heavy tackle at an unseen quarry that may not even be there, there is something almost childishly fascinating about the opportunity to return to the basics, to observe fish feeding on the surface, to cast something small and delicate at them (even if these qualities are largely relative), and, finally, to watch the fish smack that offering before your very eyes. Dragging streamers through frigid rivers or drifting egg patterns along their bottoms sometimes feels like fly-fishing in name only, a gussied-up version of techniques suited just as well to hardware or bait. Surface-feeding grayling, on the other hand, are meant for the fly-fisher, and there are times when no price can be put on finding them and enjoying what they have to offer.

But the cold, exotic beauty of the fish and its ability to connect one to the traditions of the fly still define only a part of the grayling's appeal, which is grounded above all else in the places where they live. As an exercise, I tried to remember a piece of grayling water that didn't mean something special to me. Let's see now. . . . We've already reminisced about the North Fork of the Big Hole and those nameless Russian streams flowing through the wilderness toward the Sea of Okhotsk, and you know how I feel about them. How about the little freshet pouring through a culvert somewhere along the Alcan Highway where I stopped after twelve straight hours of driving, hiked upstream through the brush, and caught grayling the size of my hand until I knew it was safe to hit the road again? Surviving the trip might not have been possible without the relief that tiny stream afforded. Then there were any number of wilderness southwest Alaska rivers where the grayling were incidental to the pursuit of moose or caribou with the bow; but even though the bugs and the weather were often difficult, I would gladly be back on any one of those rivers tomorrow if circumstances allowed. How about the lake high in the Kenai Mountains that Sheli and I hiked through the rain for hours to reach one summer day? Nick was just a baby then and I carried him on my back the whole way, and when we reached the lake the wind was blowing so hard we could think of nothing but shelter and survival. But then the front passed at last and the evening light filled up the cirque behind the lake and the grayling started to rise right next to the shoreline where we could cast to them. Before we were through, even the baby was having fun.

Appreciating grayling finally distills down to appreciating the nature of places like these. There is no reason why anyone should be enthralled by the roar of a float plane's engine or the smell of mosquito repellent or the need to secure camp against bears, but if you are not, you may never understand why people like me are fascinated by grayling. That fascination cannot depend on the kind of running and jumping provided by the subjects of other chapters in this book, for grayling on the end of a fly line are little more than overdressed shiners. At least that's the cynical view, and if you graded the species examined in this collection by some sort of computer model that integrated strength and endurance and tenacity, there is no doubt that the grayling would come out somewhere near the bottom. But not even the toniest of the glamour species inhabit such wild and wonderful places to the exclusion of all others. The grayling belongs to the realm of northern lights and midnight sun; to those of us who also feel a sense of refuge there, these circumstances alone are reason enough to care about them.

In country such as this, just one fish taken on a dry fly can change the memory of the day forever, and therein lies the final measure of the grayling's appeal.

FOURTEEN

THE ARISTOCRATS

Brook Trout: *Salvelinus fontinalis*

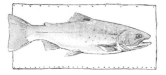

A BASIC TENET of true wilderness exploration: Garner as much information as possible *before* you bail out into the unknown. In this case, my intelligence gathering consisted of an hour-long conversation with some guy I met in a bar in a small town in northern Ontario. It was a hot summer night and we had both been drinking lots of beer, but he seemed to know what he was talking about. That's just the kind of thing you think you can get away with when you're young and foolish.

His directions had been clear enough, considering the amount of good cheer flowing through the bar: Get on the train to James Bay with your canoes. Tell them to let you out at mile such and such. Portage west a mile or two (or three or four) until you hit the river. Canoe downstream sixty miles or thereabouts until you float back under the railroad track. Then get out and flag down the next train.

And the fish? Speckled trout, brookies, squaretails. Call them what you will; the river was full of them. And yes, they were all as long as your arm. Honest.

So now the four of us were standing there watching the train chug away north toward James Bay. It was extremely quiet except for the welcoming committee of mosquitoes. We had no maps. The muskeg stretched away impassively in all directions and there wasn't a landmark in sight. I was trying not to think too hard about the strange looks the railroad crew had given us when I told them where we wanted to get out. Susan looked ready for anything as usual, but Dick and David were already exchanging looks that meant *What has Thomas gotten us into now?* Sensing a leadership crisis in the making, I made a great display of consulting my compass as if its needle could point to brook trout as surely as it could point to magnetic north. Finally there was nothing left to do but shoulder the canoes and make the great leap of faith.

It was a hot afternoon and the mosquitoes were as bad as they get. Our mysterious river was supposed to run parallel to the railroad track, so no complex navigation feats were required as long as we kept ourselves hiking in a straight line. But as the fictional George Smiley was fond of pointing out, data is no more valuable than its source, and I found it increasingly painful to remember the number of LaBatt's bottles sitting on the bar as I debriefed my mysterious informant.

After a mile or so, Dick declared a rest stop and announced that he would climb a tree to try to get some bearings toward the river. Then he shinnied up one of the monotonously similar little tamaracks, which bowed gently toward the muskeg beneath his weight. "What did you see up there?" Susan asked.

"Tamaracks and mosquitoes," Dick replied.

With a singular lack of conviction, I mumbled something about the going getting tough and the tough getting going, and then we picked up the canoes and the backpacks and set off once more toward the west through the increasingly horrible muskeg. At least the mosquitoes were having a good time.

By the time we made our next rest stop, I realized that we had not seen any ground dry enough to camp on since we left the railroad track. Cruel images began to surface in my imagination: a bar full of French-Canadians howling at the ease with which they had sent the crazy Americans to their deaths by mosquito, a stony-faced railway conductor telling the authorities: "Hey, that's where they *wanted* to get out." Then we stumbled into a little perimeter of brush and when we emerged on the other side, the river was right there in front of us.

Our initial elation did not last long. The sad fact was that our river wasn't much of a river at all. The current was so sluggish that you had to look carefully to tell which way it was flowing, and with proper motivation any of us could have spit across it. It meandered about as if it fully intended to take its time on the way to James Bay, and blow-downs lay across it as far as I could see downstream, which promised to make our progress even more tedious and miserable once we got under way. This was beginning to look less like a fishing trip than a cheap remake of *The African Queen.*

Sweating profusely, we sat down on a log for a streamside confer-ence. Our choices were to retrace our steps, camp by the railroad track, and swat mosquitoes for three days until the next southbound train came down the line or to push off downstream, trying not to remem-ber that we didn't really know where the river went, assuming that it went anywhere at all. By a unanimous four-to-zero vote, we elected to go for it.

We spent that evening and most of the next day paddling and haul-ing our fully loaded canoes across the fallen logs that littered the stream's course like jackstraws. Late that second afternoon, two large tributary creeks joined us. The stream began to open up and move, and the current underneath us finally began to look like trout water. We made camp that night on the little strip of high ground that formed the riverbank. After dinner, I excused myself and waded out into the stream below camp. Several casts later, something substantial flashed behind the streamer and I knew we had reached brook trout water at last.

Rain was falling in sheets when we woke up the next morning, and by unstated mutual agreement we each burrowed deeper into our sleep-ing bag and tried to let the weather pass. It was still raining at noon when I got out to check the canoes. The water had risen a foot or so and picked up enough color to make fishing futile. We were already camped on high ground, and since we were in no hurry we decided to stay put and wait out the storm.

Rain was still falling that evening as Susan and I cooked noodles on the gas stove at the entrance to our backpack tent and invited Dick and David over for dinner. We all sat around inside the little tent and slurped down food as the northern summer's dull-gray twilight faded from the sky, certain that the storm would cost us nothing more than a day's fishing.

The rain fell relentlessly all night and it was still raining at first light the next morning. I got up and dragged the canoes the rest of the way up the bank. The river had risen at least three feet overnight. Back inside the increasingly confining tent, Susan and I ate crackers for breakfast and read until we couldn't stand it anymore. Then we invited Dick and David over for bridge. The first several rubbers went smoothly but then the inevitable tension of having four wet people packed into a tiny tent began to take its toll. Susan made a stupid bid and when I thoughtlessly pointed this out to everyone, she announced that she was leaving me. *Just where do think you're going to go?* I wanted to know *Anywhere!* she snapped back. *Spending the night in the rain would be better than spending another night with you!* She bundled up her sleeping bag angrily and stormed across the campsite to the other tent, where she spent the next two days while the rain kept pouring down from the sky. I believe it was then I realized that, despite her wonderful qualities as an outdoor companion, Susan and I would not be spending the rest of our lives together.

Late in the afternoon of the third day we powwowed under a spruce tree next to the riverbank and declared officially that we were in trouble. Tethered to the highest available trees, the canoes were about to float through camp. The flood water was less than a foot away from spilling over the bank and we were already on the highest ground in the area. We agreed to take shifts during the night to monitor the water levels, although it was not entirely clear what we would do if the river decided to come after us. Then suddenly the rain began to falter and blue sky emerged overhead and we knew we were going to make it.

The water crested late that night under Dick's watchful eye, and early the next morning we broke camp and launched the canoes into the angry river. Fishing was out of the question. We asked nothing of the water now other than that it take us downstream to the railroad track without eating us for dessert. We paddled down the swollen river all morning, and by early afternoon we could feel the water retracting. Then we glided around a bend and ran right into the New Yorkers.

It's always startling to come across people unexpectedly in the wilderness, especially when you've been in the bush long enough to let yourself enjoy the fiction that you and the members of your own party are the only humans left on earth. A trapper or a wilderness surveyor would have been enough of a surprise; the New Yorkers were beyond belief.

I never learned why or how they got where they were. There were three of them, a father and two sons, and it was obvious that things were not going well. The youngest of the boys seemed oblivious to their situation. The older boy was trying hard to maintain some kind of order. I admired him at once and like to imagine that he went on to become a good woodsman one day. Their father had lost it completely. He was sprawled in front of a lifeless fire listening to static on a transistor radio. Fragments of camping gear lay scattered up and down the bank and everyone looked as if they had been out in the elements for a while.

We pulled the canoes in to what was left of their camp to check everyone's vital signs. No one seemed in any immediate danger. The father asked how we planned to get out of there. I told him, and invited them to canoe downriver with us. He pointed to their battered canoe and said he didn't think they could do that, and I didn't argue with him. I suggested that he hike back to the railroad tracks and wait for the next train and he said that he had been considering that. Then he asked me which way the railroad tracks were. I pointed east and he rose and set off into the muskeg.

Matters were clearly out of control. Dick grabbed him before he could lose himself in the featureless tamarack jungle. We asked him what he planned to do with his equipment and he said he was going to leave it right where it was. We finally got everyone organized into a column of sorts, took a compass bearing, and set off across country carrying their gear on our shoulders. When we finally came upon the track three miles later, he fell down on it as if he could not bear the thought of ever being away from at least some small vestige of civilization again.

The four of us hiked back through the scrubby trees to what we had begun to call the River from Hell and set off downstream once more. Three days later, we rode the last of the high water around a bend and there was the railroad trestle overhead. I had not taken my fly rod out of its case since the second evening of the trip.

It took us more than an hour to haul all our gear up the bank, and then we sat down and waited and tried not to wonder too hard about whether or not we had the right day for a southbound train or what we would do if the train didn't stop. Then the tracks began to hum at last and the sound of the first internal combustion engine we had heard in a week rose from around the bend. The engine had already slowed to a crawl by the time it drew abreast of us and there right next to the engineer were the New Yorkers, waving joyously as they passed.

As they helped us load our canoes into an open boxcar, the father explained that the first train to come along had been the northbound freight and they had taken it. Now rested, fed, and refreshed, they bore little resemblance to the bedraggled trio we had rescued from the flooded river earlier in the week. Once we were under way again, the father led us back to the dining car where he threw down some bills and told the waiter to bring us anything we wanted. And he did.

Susan and I were buddies again by the time we fell asleep to the rhythm of the rails gliding by beneath. So was everyone else on the train, as best I can recall. That's when I realized that this had really been a classic brook trout expedition after all, for that is the way it is with the very best of fishing.

When it's really good, you don't even need the fish.

I grew up with brook trout on my mind. While my first fly-caught trout was a brown, my first trout, period, was a brookie, and it was no less of an accomplishment for having been taken with garden hackle. Somewhere near the outskirts of Boston there used to be a place called Mann's Pond. (Perhaps it still exists, but I can't imagine a place like that surviving all those years' worth of development, and I'm not curious enough to go back East and look for it.) Ike was barely president when I discovered Mann's Pond and its wealth of frogs and tadpoles and other forms of aquatic life. I was fishing for shiners there one evening when something struck my worm with more authority than I had ever experienced before. Moments later I was clutching a fish so compelling that I ran all the way back home to show it to my father. He inspected the catch gravely and declared to my immense satisfaction that I had probably caught the first and only *Salvelinus fontinalis* ever taken from Mann's Pond. I didn't know quite what he was talking about, but I sensed somehow that my life would never be quite the same again. Sure enough, it wasn't.

In a sense, the brook trout occupies a similar position for all of us, forming a sort of collective historical pole toward which the compass of

American fly-fishing ultimately points. The development of our cultural traditions seems analogous to fossils stratified in layers of rock, with the oldest levels of everything buried on the East Coast and newer and newer layers appearing as you travel west until you get to Southern California, where things are so hysterically new that some haven't even happened yet. This principle certainly holds true for fly-fishing. There were plenty of trout found out West, of course, but for the first hundred years of our country's existence westerners were too busy trying to stay alive to worry about having fun catching pretty fish. The whole notion of sportfishing requires a certain degree of civilization, leisure time, and the luxury of considering matters other than day-to-day survival. In the New World for most of the last century, such conditions were met only on the east coast of America, which is why our fly-fishing traditions are so firmly grounded in Atlantic salmon and brook trout, aristocratic species well intended for what is a fundamentally unnecessary (even if immensely satisfying) pursuit.

To get a feel for all this, it helps to open an older fishing text to the chapter on fly patterns and take a look at the illustrations. (How old is old? I hate to say it, but anything published much before my own birth will do. Try an early edition of Ray Bergman's *Trout,* for example.) The plates will be dominated by Cretaceous-looking relics called wet flies. There will be hundreds and hundreds of them, most gaudy, some beautiful. One can imagine what an absolute blast they were to tie entirely from natural materials, and to fish to trout dumb enough to strike them. They carry names like Montreal and Parmachene Belle and bear a striking resemblance to absolutely nothing familiar to the modern fly-fisher, which is of course responsible for much of their charm. And they owe their place in history to the brook trout.

Actually, the notion that classic brook-trout flies are purely abstract expressions of the fly-tyer's art is not quite accurate. Some resemble subsurface nymphs in an Impressionist way that could have been entirely accidental. And because brook trout were known to strike hooks baited with brook-trout fins, of all things, that color scheme is well represented in early wet-fly patterns as well. Since the brook trout's pectoral fin is one of the most beautiful visual compositions to be found anywhere in nature, there seems little harm in that. It's still great fun to imagine a pair of our turn-of-the-century predecessors studying the water intently and trying to decide between a Scarlet Ibis and a Royal Coachman. Just think how far we've come. I guess.

Brook trout were an integral part of my outdoor childhood in Upstate New York, not least because they were just about the only show in town when it came to fly-fishing. Almost all the tiny streams around our rural home had a few brookies in them. They were small and it took a lot of work to catch them, not because they were smart but because the streams were choked with brush and there weren't all that many trout in them anyway. They were still fun to catch.

Once or twice a year, my father and his friends would head north to the Adirondacks or Canada for a wilderness trip in search of more and bigger brook trout. I soon learned that doing my chores and remaining in my mother's good graces was the secret to getting to go along on those expeditions, an exercise in motivation that was no doubt what my cagey parents had in mind all along. Well, it worked. We caught nice brook trout on some of those trips, and I can remember three- and four-pounders that I would still be willing to hike an awful long way for a chance at today. Those trips also taught me much about the value of truly wild places, a principle that would serve me well throughout my adult life. I suppose it was the memory of the solitude and the hook-jawed brookies I had in mind the day I talked Susan and Dick and David into the float down the River from Hell. Oh, well. We realized part of the promise.

Brookies don't really belong out West, but then neither do we. The same human imperatives that led to the introduction of the rainbow and the brown here in cutthroat country produced a smattering of brook-trout fishing here beneath the Big Sky, where the fish in question are always referred to officially as Eastern Brook Trout, as if there are western ones too (there aren't). At least this formal designation serves to remind us that brook trout are dudes in the last analysis.

Don't let such condescension fool you. Out here, brook trout do best in out-of-the-way little streams that promise respite from Blue Ribbon crowds. Lots of us here have favorites. The identity of such streams tends to remain classified under the heading "Local Knowledge," right along with the location of morel patches, elk wallows, and the secret springs that mallards frequent during the late waterfowl season. Don't think for one minute that I'm going to risk my own security clearance just because somebody paid me to write a book. Coming out to fish Montana? Try the Big Horn. I hear it's been great lately.

Fish people also learned to appreciate the brook trout's hardiness when it came time to dump a barrelful of something into barren alpine lakes and see what survived. Once those little Darwinian pots had been stirred a time or two, the transplanted brookie often came out on top, which explains the little pockets of brook trout (Excuse me, *Eastern* Brook Trout) scattered around the mountain West.

You find them in the damnedest places. On a bowhunt above timberline in the middle of nowhere a few years back, I returned to camp frustrated and beat at the end of the day and cast a fly out into the lake next to camp just because I couldn't think of anything better to do. I was fishing a weighted streamer, and the scenery around the lake was so gorgeous that I almost forgot about the fly as it sank down into the lucid depths of the lake. Suddenly something struck, and then I saw the vivid colors of a brook trout as the fish took the fight to the surface. It was no token specimen, either, but a solid sixteen-incher that packed enough punch to make me worry about my knot. When the fish finally came to rest in the shallows, I stared at that unexpected bouquet of orange and green and white as if I had been hypnotized. I was suddenly a kid again, and if I had been struck dead at that very moment I probably would have said "Brook Trout" the way Orson Welles said "Rosebud" in *Citizen Kane.*

That is the essential quality of true aristocrats. They travel well and demonstrate a consistency of class and style no matter where you find them. Just knowing that they may show up at any moment is enough to make you want to look and act your best, and having done so, it's not always necessary that they bother to show up at all. Even in their absence, the thought of them can be enough to enrich our lives.

FIFTEEN

A TALE OF TWO PONDS

Largemouth Bass: *Micropterus salmoides*
White Crappie: *Pomoxis annularis*

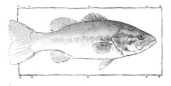

I T TOOK SEVERAL ATTEMPTS just to find The Bass Pond, but finding the good places is never easy.

The first time we set out to fish it, the directions I had been given proved incomprehensible. Landmarks never appeared where they were supposed to be and back roads wandered off hopelessly into the sage. Ray and I bounced around the prairie for hours making note of the places where we saw bird cover and antelope, but the only water we found was a tiny stock pond that could not possibly have been the fish-rich reservoir described by local rumor.

The second time we went in search of The Bass Pond, we left town under clear skies, but an afternoon thunderstorm sprang up out of the prairie and dropped half an inch of rain onto the thirsty ground. That turned the back roads into tenacious brown gumbo and we were lucky to make it back to the highway without spending the night marooned in the sagebrush. By the time we hit pavement again, my pickup looked like it had participated in an amphibious assault. The truck shed chunks of dried mud for days, and every time one fell from the axles, the noise reminded me of just what lengths one will go to in order to catch bass in trout country.

Today I have set off by myself on another attempt at discovery. I have obtained a revised set of directions from the rancher who owns the place, a personal friend. Of course, nothing guarantees that these will be any more intelligible than the first version. Turkey season is over, however, and the creek is between hatches, and I just can't imagine a better time to search out the increasingly mythical source of all those bass.

I depart home before dawn because the quest for a spring gobbler with the bow has left me accustomed to rising early, and the sunrises have been so invigorating lately that I don't think I can stand to miss one. Besides, I have been in a pensive mood lately, and no circumstance does justice to that frame of mind quite like a prairie sunrise. As I drive east from town toward the rolling country where The Bass Pond allegedly awaits, the morning is little more than an abstract glow off in the distance. By the time I leave the county road, though, colors have started to creep into the landscape, and when I get out to open the first gate, the smell of sage sweeps over me like a wave, justifying every measure of inconvenience my early departure demanded.

Sagebrush and bass make a curious combination. Hardly anyone thinks of bass—largemouths, in this case—as a prairie species, and they aren't supposed to be. Bass fishing is expected to evoke images of lily pads and dragonflies and languid summer days, not wind and raptors and cactus. There are more hard edges here than a lifetime of bass fishing is supposed to contain. No wonder we've been having all this trouble just figuring out where we're supposed to go.

To the unappreciative eye, the prairie seems like a barren place, but that is an illusion. Savannah habitat is the most productive in the world, and our own Great Plains are no exception. Of course you can't tell that to the tourists hurrying across eastern Montana on their way to the stuff that looks like what they have come to expect from the books and the movies, but that's their problem.

Today's first hour of light provides plenty of support for this thesis. With the gate behind me, the rolling terrain comes alive as I drive on ahead with my revised set of written directions spread out beside me on the seat. There are indeed antelope just as the sagebrush promised, and as the herd speeds effortlessly along beside the truck, their new spring coats of white and tan look like pastel paint in the spreading flood of daylight. A mule-deer buck stands silhouetted on a nearby ridge with the morning light behind him. His developing velvet antlers are still short and chunky, but they suggest enough potential to make me file away the sight in my preseason compendium of bowhunting data Meadowlarks are everywhere, flushing before the truck in little bursts of gold, and at the second gate I pause and shut off the engine just to hear them sing. It seems impossible for all that volume to come from something so insubstantial. The naturalist inside says that there should be an explanation for the meadowlark's vocal ability and that I should be able to deduce it, but a wiser impulse suggests that I just shut up and listen, and that is the one I finally heed.

Under way again, I pass the site of an apparent wrong turn on our first exploratory trip and proceed with renewed confidence. Matching the configuration of backroads to my written directions is still no easy task, but after another half-dozen miles, I crest one final ridge and look down into the next coulee, and there is The Bass Pond at last.

I wind carefully down the hill, cross the weathered earthen dam, and stop to survey my find. It's a large body of water by the standards of the area's stock ponds, a good five hundred yards long and nearly half that wide. The water is clear, although given the confluence of washed-out gullies at its upper end, it would probably need a few days to settle down after a heavy rain. The shoreline is largely barren, but there is one patch of reeds that could support a duck blind, another bit of intelligence promptly filed away for future reference. The waterfowl that flushed upon my arrival are still circling overhead as they try to decide whether to ignore me or withdraw to the next pond, wherever that may be. There is a squadron of divers overhead in addition to the usual Central Flyway smorgasbord of puddleducks, and as they dip low over the water and catch the morning sun with their primaries, I can identify them as redheads. A flock of avocets stirs at the far edge of the pond, and a yellowlegs joins them in scolding my intrusion. I just stand and watch for a minute or two, and by the time I begin to extract my fishing gear from the truck everything has grown accustomed to my presence. No one ever asks anything unreasonable of you out here, which is one reason I love the prairie so much.

I have parked the truck in the natural place to park trucks, and the presence of old bootprints in the dirt helps confirm that I have found the right pond after all. A half-dozen beer cans lie scattered about the ground to remind me what pricks people can be, as if I need reminding. I retrieve the cans and hurl them angrily into the back of the pickup, and the clatter they make as they hit the metal bed is almost enough to destroy the spell of the place. I make a point to breathe slowly and listen to the birds as I run the line through the rod's guides, and by the time this simple task is completed I am ready to go fishing.

The sun is warming the prairie already, so I leave my waders in the truck. Waders are for trout streams; this is bass water (I hope), the kind that invites you to let the mud squish between your toes as you wade it wet. Old running shoes and cut-off blue jeans can serve no higher purpose. Down at the waterline, I poke through my junk box looking for something suitable to put on the end of the leader. There's very little science involved in my occasional forays into the realm of warm-water fly-fishing, and the selection of flies usually depends heavily on beaten-up versions of gaudy patterns once meant for something else. Here in the bottom of the box, however, are a couple of genuine bass poppers that I probably crafted as a kid. They look like fossils with their rusted hooks and frayed feathers and crumbly cork bodies, but the one that was once meant to look like a frog now looks like just what The Bass Pond had in mind all along.

I move to the pond's eastern shore to get the light behind me and dig my polarized glasses from their case. This is unknown water, and I want to see everything that happens out there if I can. The popper is a bit bulky for my 5-weight rod, but after a false cast or two the syncopation needed to keep things moving begins to feel natural. Finally, there is nothing left to do but start fishing.

It has been thirty years since I moved West and left the bass in my life behind. In Alaska, warm-water gamefish scarcely exist. In Montana, there aren't a lot of them to be found and they don't get much respect when they are, which represents a foolish and unfortunate bias of the very sort that gives fly-fishers their often deserved reputation as snots. Trout are fish, not golden calves; the fact that they're fun to catch was never meant to impugn the reputation of other species. It's easy to lose track of this principle here in Montana, not in the least because trout have gotten themselves all intertwined with money, which is the sort of development that really bothers people like me. It takes me twenty casts or so this morning to work all this through, by which time I realize that

I am perilously close to letting a simple fishing trip turn into some kind of political statement. Fortunately, the first strike occurs just in time to save the morning from such a corrupt fate.

One moment the worn cork frog is making its way across the water's polished surface and then it's gone, consumed by a strike no trout could ever make, not even in its wildest dreams. Whatever has taken it has done so with a slurp that sounds like a child trying to eat spaghetti. The noise and the sight of the strike remind me that it is the commotion largemouths make that is the essence of catching them. Fishing for bass below the surface seems to miss the point in a way that goes beyond even the wet-fly–dry-fly conflicts that arise in the pursuit of trout. This morning, the pond is so still, the strike so abrupt. This is what I have come for.

The fish does well for its size after the strike, but it weighs only a pound or thereabouts, so there's no reason to try to turn this into more than it is. Still, the fish is worth savoring up close, if only because catching a black bass is such an exceptional event now that I no longer live where they do. One creek north of town contains a few little ones, and in the summer the kids like to go up and float it in innertubes and catch bass and shoot the rattlesnakes that abound along its banks, which as outings go is about as much fun as it sounds and certainly not something I can do more than once a season. In terms of bass fishing, that was about it for us, at least until I got wind of The Bass Pond, all of which explains why the one-pound largemouth resting in my hand is the occasion of such delight, even though real bass enthusiasts would scarcely give my fish a second look.

The fish is spiny, chunky, and substantial in a way no trout will ever be. Its sides are rough to the touch and it wears an in-your-face look befitting a species that isn't afraid to eat other vertebrates half its size for lunch if it comes to that. The bass has certainly tagged the popper with a vengeance, and by the time I've backed the hook out of its jaw my poor cork frog looks as if it has about exhausted its useful lifespan. Of course that's not the kind of thing you can go around brooding over.

That fish is just the first, if not of many then at least of quite a few, especially considering that it was far from clear that there were any fish to be found here, period. I have heard rumors of three- and four-pound fish in The Bass Pond, but these rumors hail from the same source as my directions and are probably about as reliable. Even by the end of the morning I've seen no fish that comes close to confirming them. A few one-pound-plus specimens will have to suffice for size, and they do. The cork frog is retired forever and my one other real bass popper doesn't survive its third fish, but it turns out that a heavily greased Muddler Minnow jerked along through the surface film does just as well. At least I get to see and hear each fish take it with a slurp, and that's enough to confirm that I am really bass fishing, no matter what the experts might say.

Emboldened by my success at The Bass Pond, we embark two weeks later on a similar mission in search of crappies.

Ray and I have the kids with us this time: Nick, Jenny, and Joe. This just sounds like the kind of project likely to go better with kids, a picnic lunch, and a few cold beers, and sure enough, it is. A rancher friend has told us about the pond out behind his place. He stocked it with crappies a year or so ago and now it's full of the rascals, which have grown big enough to be worth catching. They'll hit only one thing, he has assured us with conspiratorial sincerity: a crappie fly of his own secret invention, which turns out to be a scaled-down version of the familiar rubber-legged Girdle Bug. So I've tied up a box full of this infallible pattern and loaded the cooler with everything we needed to load it with, and now it is time for yet another adventure in the unheralded warm-water fisheries of the eastern Montana prairie.

This time the directions are easy enough, but when we bounce over the last rise and take a good, hard look at what can only be The Crappie Pond, there is a collective sinking of the spirits that even the kids find impossible to ignore. In contrast to The Bass Pond, this one is small and decidedly uninspiring. The water is dingy and weed-choked. Cattle have pounded down the banks and left the stink of their droppings hanging in the sultry air. Overhead, the sun is beating down intently, which of course is not the pond's fault, but the effect is to suggest snakes and bugs and general misery nonetheless.

But here we are, and the best approach to such situations is almost always to set up the rods and go fishing. Joe and Nick are old enough to be their own independent strike force, and there is nothing to be done about them but to stand back. Jenny still needs help getting started, which I provide her as Ray rummages cheerfully through the cooler containing the beer. The boys are being smart-asses as usual, and they turn up their noses at my carefully dressed crappie flies, which is their privilege. I tie one on for Jenny and then sit down out of harm's way. It is time to let the show begin.

The Crappie Pond makes a perfect target for a kid Jenny's age, and with no brush to deal with on her backcast she soon has the miniature Girdle Bug twitching its way back through the weeds as if she's been practicing this all week. Suddenly the rod tip comes alive in a burst of activity, and it doesn't seem possible that one eight-year-old girl can squeal as long and as loudly as she does. There is little elegance to the fight, which consists for the most part of Jenny's hoisting the fish toward shore along with a bridal train of weeds, and then she dives forward into the mud and the cow shit and smothers her quarry like a linebacker recovering a fumble.

Subdued and envious, the boys approach as she raises the fish in triumph. They are trout kids, and none of them has ever seen a crappie before. It looks as exotic to them as my Mann's Pond brook trout once looked to me. The three of them examine and admire the fish and the boys even allow themselves to admit a grudging touch of respect for Jenny's accomplishment. There is some nattering over the fly, but it's not the kind of day to be teaching anybody lessons in humility, so I place the box of Girdle Bugs at everyone's disposal.

The boys change flies and turn their attention back to the water while Jenny and I have a talk. I explain that it's her fish, and that she must now make the choice between releasing it to fight again or killing it and taking it home to eat. Kill it and eat it, she declares in no uncertain terms, and since there is no biological contraindication to this verdict, I accept it despite my reservations about how anything spawned in this mud hole might actually taste. Then Jenny proudly carries her crappie back up the bank to the cooler, where Ray is busy making room for her catch twelve fluid ounces at a time.

Now that they're properly equipped with real crappie flies, the two boys are soon fast to fish as well. By the time Jenny has taken her third, it's obvious that she needs no more help from me, and since everyone seems to be having so much fun with all this, I dig out my 3-weight rod and have at it myself. And it turns out that the kids are right: It *is* fun. By the time we're done, the cooler is full of crappies and we're all covered with rich black mud that coats us like tar and stinks to high heaven, although nobody seems to care. Back at the truck, the kids pick up every last vestige of litter without having to be told to do so, which reassures me that they have been raised right after all. Then we set off for home, where in a matter of hours we'll discover that crappies rolled in cornmeal and fried in a hot skillet taste just great no matter what the circumstances of their upbringing.

I am certainly no authority on taking fish from fresh warm water on the fly. This should come as no surprise; I haven't spent much time in and about fresh warm water, and in contrast to saltwater flats, the fish that live there do not excite me enough to make me go far out of my way to fish for them. This admission is intended as a comment on my personal priorities and not on the fish themselves, which no doubt have a great deal to offer even to the most experienced anglers. I have simply chosen to deal with these species on simpler terms, and I mean to imply no disrespect for them in the process. Those who wish to read something on this subject written with proper authority are referred to *Bass on the Fly* by A. D. Livingston, who both knows his subject intimately and writes about it well, a conjunction of events that occurs less frequently in outdoor-writing circles than most practitioners of the form would like to admit.

With all that said, there must be some reason why an angler living near the country's best trout water would turn his back on all those famous streams and venture into the prairie to fish for undersized versions of species that seldom draw more than a polite nod in fly-fishing circles under the best of circumstances. One explanation is that your correspondent is either a sociopath or a fool (or both); since you have made it this far, we can assume that you have either dismissed this possibility or come to terms with it. Another is that these fish have more to offer on the end of a fly rod than the conventional wisdom of a sometimes stuffy sport is willing to concede, and this much is certainly correct. Finally comes the notion that variety of experience is intrinsically worthwhile, that one should always pay heed to the idea of doing different things just because they are different, and that it's always admirable to catch fish just because they're there. This may be the most intriguing explanation of them all.

In the case of bass and panfish, I find that the idea of fishing gets all wound up with the ideas of childhood and maturity. These are the kinds of fish I often fished for when I was young, and making the effort to do so again, even on a limited scale, offers the chance to reflect upon that childhood and what it meant to me. On the good days, I even get to experience some of its wonders again, through my children's eyes if not quite through my own. In the process, the significance of those fish that strike with noisy slurps cannot be defined by weights and livewells and fish finders and all the other trappings of bass tournaments, those ultimately obscene exercises in the corruption of innocence that sometimes make me wonder if there is anything people will not do to make a buck.

One thing is for sure: None of that is the fault of the fish. While I will probably never do what it takes to experience the kind of fishing that makes serious bass anglers lose sleep at night, I can still enjoy these warm-water species for what they are to me: an excuse to watch a prairie sunrise or to roll joyously in the mud.

SIXTEEN

REDS

Sockeye Salmon: *Oncorhynchus nerka*

JULY HAS PEAKED ON THE KENAI and the crowds have started to thin. A little bit of real darkness has crept back into the middle of the night, but the days are still long enough to leave those of us who love the outdoors a bit giddy. The skies have been clear and calm for nearly a week now, which only adds to the general sense of rapture. The kings are all but gone, but it's too nice a day to do anything but go fishing, so when I return home from work I change clothes and head straight to the river. For better or worse, it is time to fish for red salmon.

Upstream, the long sunny days have gone to work on the glacier's exposed flanks, and now the river is feeling its muscles. The banks fly past as I run the boat downstream with all of the current's authority behind me. A half-dozen boats are anchored along the Red Salmon Hole, which doesn't bother me in the least. If I needed solitude today, I would have hiked up into the mountains or fired up the Cub and flown somewhere across the inlet. This is a different matter entirely.

Falling into place unobtrusively at the end of the line, I study the water and there they are. The visibility in the silted Kenai is too limited to reveal actual schools of fish, but migrating reds porpoise on the surface with an unmistakable comma-shaped rise form, and now the Red Salmon Hole is boiling with them. Paradoxically, this intelligence fills me with an odd despair known only to veteran red-salmon anglers.

Upstream, the occupants of the other boats seem to be having a good time. While some are casting conventional spinners and spoons, the lure of choice seems to be a local favorite that I've christened the Kenai Coachman, a 3/0 treble hook with an ounce or two of lead molded to the shank. Pitched across the current with heavy spinning gear and retrieved through the schooled fish with a series of vigorous jerks, this rig is designed, as an old-time Alaskan friend once explained, "to encourage the bastards to bite." Snagging is illegal in Alaska now, but this injunction is widely ignored and almost impossible to enforce. Whatever discomfort the goings-on upstream may arouse is tempered by the fact that the boats are all local and their occupants are mostly friends and neighbors. Just as they have made peace with me and my fly rod over the years, there should be no real reason for me not to make peace with their own time-honored means of obtaining their winter's supply of fish. In this country, you can always make an argument for trying to get along.

I run the leader through the rod's guides, reach for my fly book, and discover that I have inadvertently brought my saltwater belly bag with me instead of the one that contains my salmon gear. As I stare blankly at the neat little rows of Snapping Shrimp and Crazy Charlies and listen to the salmon splash, a wonderful, liberating thought occurs to me: It doesn't matter!

The reason it doesn't matter is that fishing for migrating red salmon is a free-fall exercise in the absurd. No one knows much about why Pacific salmon strike in fresh water to begin with, but reds elevate these uncertainties to an art form. Even in salt water, reds live on crustaceans too small to be imitated by much of anything, which accounts for their negligible sporting significance at sea. In fresh water, the process of hooking one on rod and reel can become almost totally irrational. When sockeyes returned to Seattle's Lake Washington some years back, swarms of anglers tried almost every lure known in order to determine the most effective means of catching them. The winner? A bare hook. This is not the sort of conclusion likely to endear the red salmon to enthusiasts of the fly-tyer's art.

If they were truly consistent and never hit anything, there wouldn't be much of a problem. We could simply ignore them the way we ignore the federal deficit and go on about our lives as if they had never arrived from the sea. For better or worse, however, red salmon do strike flies and lures frequently enough to keep us from pretending that it can't be done. To make matters more confusing, at certain times and in certain places they do so with enthusiasm, although they are more likely to strike just often enough to keep you from saying the hell with it forever. Barely.

By now the obvious question should have reared its ugly head in the mind of any serious fly-fisher unfamiliar with *Oncorhynchus nerka*, which is: Why bother?

Several excuses come to mind. Although a relative lightweight among Pacific salmon, averaging six or eight pounds as a rule, reds pack plenty of punch on their lightweight frames. Per unit weight, fresh reds may well be the hottest of them all on the end of a fly line (assuming you can get them there in the first place). They are an aesthetic masterpiece of design, and they usually retain their bright saltwater sheen far longer than the pinks and dogs that will soon follow them inland. And if you feel like keeping a fish for a salmon dinner (both a biologically and a politically correct option, since reds, like all Pacific salmon, do not survive their spawning run), there is nothing to rival a sockeye on the table.

And, finally, there are almost always a lot of them, which can be either an asset or a liability depending on both the salmon's mood and your own. There are certainly a lot of them out there in front of me right now. Upstream, no one seems to be catching much except for an occasional connection by one of the snaggers, but the Red Salmon Hole is full of fish and here I sit without so much as a single official sockeye fly in my possession.

Undaunted, I study my bonefish fly book and select a Crazy Charlie, which when you get right down to it seems every bit as logical a choice as anything from my missing salmon belly bag. At least I'm fishing, I tell myself as I work the fly out over the water. At least the phone isn't ringing and the wind isn't blowing, and the mosquitoes aren't even on the prowl. Alaska can be a difficult country, and up here the wise outdoorsperson learns to appreciate the little things no matter what the mood of the fish.

The river is considerably higher than it was in king season, but reds don't hug the bottom the way their big brothers do, and the technical problems of getting a fly down to the fish are not as great as they were back then despite the powerful current. It is important to realize that you're not fishing bottom structure now, that the river is just a cold, wet highway for all those fish as they move upstream to the spawning grounds. The object of the game is simply to get the fly out into the flow of traffic. If you can't come to terms with this concept, fly-fishing glacial rivers will drive you crazy, and it will be only a matter of time until the snaggers' technique starts to look more and more inviting, if only as a form of well-deserved revenge.

But it hasn't yet come to that, and with luck it never will. At least there will be no such crisis of conscience today, for on the fourth or fifth cast, just as I'm finally getting a measure of the current, the rod tip goes down hard and I am fast to a red salmon.

We might as well acknowledge up front that if you drag enough flies through enough tightly schooled fish, you're going to foul-hook a few of them even without the aid of a Kenai Coachman. There will come times when such an event may not seem entirely undesirable. After a typical hour or two of frustration at the hands of red salmon determined not be taken according to the rules of fair chase, values sometimes start to feel quite relative indeed. Do this often enough and you may begin to wonder just how bad hooking a red salmon in the butt section can be, especially if, you know, it happens pretty much by accident and you release the fish at the end of the fight in accordance with the law. In a rare victory for advocates of the moral high ground, it doesn't work that way. Fish hooked in the dorsal fin or the tail (which is where misplaced flies usually wind up) are absolutely no fun, even if all this really did happen by chance and you have every intention of being honorable and letting the fish go when it's over. Foul-hooked salmon wallow and set their sides against the current and take forever to bring to hand, and manage in the process to do absolutely nothing that a fish is supposed to do for you on the end of a fly line. When something like that is all over and done, you just hope no one was watching.

Which is why the solid, unequivocal whack out there in the blue current feels so satisfying. The fish has actually struck the fly and there it is to prove it, jumping and turning in the sun with the leader trailing from its mouth just the way it's supposed to be. The fish heads upstream past the neighboring boats like an advertisement for my own luck, and everyone courteously holds their fire to avoid casting across the line. The salmon runs and leaps as only a red salmon can, and for a moment the pure pleasure of it is nearly unbelievable.

But what really turns out to be unbelievable is that after landing that fish, I make two more casts and hook another bright salmon fair and square. Upstream, people are starting to talk. The first one could be dismissed as the statistics of small numbers, but now it looks as if I might actually be onto something. I myself am growing uneasy. The thought of solving the mystery of migrating red salmon is almost unbearable. Perhaps I'll become famous, patent the Crazy Charlie, change its name to the Crazy Don, appear on the "Tonight" show, get rich, retire. These delusions are almost enough to ruin the pleasure of the fish on the end of the line.

It is the third fish, however, that proves impossible to ignore. Upstream, the natives grow restless. Someone ups anchor at the head of the run and I can swear I hear the words "son of a bitch" drift across the water before the outboard sputters to life. Then the boat just upstream begins to drift down toward me as gently as a lion stalking its prey, and by the time the fish is in the net, my visitors are right there beside me.

"Looks like you got 'em figured out!" someone suggests.

"Yeah, well," I mumble in reply.

They are studying the fly intently as I remove it from the fish's mouth. "What do you call that thing?" another asks.

"Um, Don's Sockeye Special," I ad-lib, holding the Crazy Charlie out for their inspection.

"Never seen a red-salmon fly like that before," my interrogator admits.

"I make 'em myself," I reply modestly, and then I pull my own anchor and drift backward out of the tail of the pool before I become unable to stand this scrutiny any longer.

That was the beginning of my brief reign as a local authority on red salmon. It was also pretty much the end. Word of such matters travels fast in small communities and for several weeks people I had never heard of called me on the phone to ask about the fly. By the time I had grown accustomed to my own celebrity, more people were calling to tell me they had tried my new fly and found it worthless. I didn't bother to argue in defense of Don's Sockeye Special, née Crazy Charlie. How could I? I hadn't caught another fish on it since that one memorable day on the Kenai.

At least it was prettier than a bare hook.

In many ways, the red salmon is Alaska's essential fish. It's certainly plentiful and good to eat, qualities that seem to define the fishing experience for most Alaskans whether they fish for business or for pleasure. I remember the summer when OPEC lost its grip and oil prices tumbled, and for the first time in memory a red salmon coming over the stern in a gill net was worth more money than a barrel of crude. That was certainly some sort of economic milestone up north. No matter how edgy the relationship between sport- and commercial-fishing interests can sometimes become, it was hard not to imagine that Alaska was a better place with its fish worth more than its fossil fuels.

Of course, commercial fishermen love red salmon. The fish are lucrative, and if you're fishing with a drift net, you don't have to worry about getting them to strike. For those of us relying on more contemplative means of take, reds can be a true enigma. And for fly-fishers accustomed to the finely tuned process of matching hatches, a stream full of fresh reds can become a prescription for anguish.

But there they are every year right on schedule, filling the gap between kings and silvers and daring you to ignore them. Reds usually arrive during nice weather, at least by Alaska standards. They are beautiful fish and they are found in beautiful places. And even if they didn't run and jump with the very best when hooked, they would be difficult to forget despite their bad manners.

As it is, well. . . .

It's later in the season and I am starting to think about silvers and caribou and ptarmigan, but all are still a few weeks away. Right now it's just me and the red salmon, about ten thousand of them as nearly as I can tell.

I am alone on a lake west of Cook Inlet, sitting on my airplane's float eating a sandwich. It is a clear, gorgeous day and the Alaska Range towers behind me, a sweeping expanse of snow and rock and alder that suggests sheer beauty to those lucky enough to see the scenery here without having to walk through it. Out in front of the beached airplane, vast schools of fish are roaring around trying to make up their minds about the little feeder stream their instincts have programmed them to ascend. These are the kind of red salmon you're supposed to be able to catch, but for the last two hours this theory has received no support from me.

The lake contains glacial silt but the little tributary is clear, and I can see the fish easily as they mill about its mouth. We are ten miles or so inland from the sea. These fish are not the mint-bright specimens encountered earlier on the lower Kenai, but they're still dressed in ocean silver rather than their scarlet and olive spawning colors, and I would like to catch a few of them. Honest.

I hear the distant drone of another airplane somewhere in the empty sky and rotate my head to fix its location. It's an ambivalent sound when you're out in the bush: discouraging if you have come for solitude but sweet music indeed if you are broken down and hurting. Today I'm pretty much neutral toward the idea of human company, as are the salmon.

This spot is not really a secret, and it's no surprise when the Cessna appears over the trees, cuts power, and drops in to join me. The aircraft belongs to a local charter operator and I know the pilot. He glides into the shallows beside me and we chat as the aircraft disgorges its cargo of vaguely worried-looking visitors. They are all overdressed in chest waders and needless rain gear, and they glance up and down the shoreline before leaving the security of the airplane as if they are certain killer grizzlies are lurking in the brush. At least no one is carrying a tourist-issue magnum in a shoulder holster. Thank God for that.

I finish my sandwich and lean back in the sun to watch them fish. You don't get to lean back in the sun much in this country, and when you do, I figure you ought to take advantage of the opportunity unless something really exciting is going on. The way things have been going here all morning, watching three other fools pound the water sounds every bit as much fun as pounding it some more myself.

"Where you been?" I inquire of the pilot, and he mentions another nearby lake. "Do any good?" I ask.

"Reds," he mutters with a shake of his head as if this says it all, and I suppose in a way it does. I feel sorry for him. These people have paid money to endure this frustration, and I have already gotten the idea that they are not the kind of people who will go home smiling and wide-eyed in wonder at the wilderness experience should the day end fishless. Encounters like this one remind me why I have so assiduously avoided the lure of the guide business, and what a genius I seem to be for having done so.

The tourists have seen the fish now, and they are casting spoons into the agitated water with grim determination, unable to believe their own inability to induce a strike from something out there. I commiserate quietly with the pilot. It is time for one last shot.

I clip off whatever disappointment remained on the end of my leader from a morning's worth of failed attempts and replace it at random with a yellow bucktail. A flat rock offers a platform from which I can fish without worrying too much about my backcast. As is usually the case when I'm fishing away from fly-rod-oriented company, my tackle draws some curious looks. Then the yellow bucktail plops down right at the junction between the stream's clear water and the lake's glacial turbidity, and before I can strip the fly twice I am improbably, impossibly fast to a fish.

While not quite as bright and spectacular as the sea-fresh specimens from the Kenai, this one is still hot enough to jump and earn some envious stares from the audience as it works its way down into my backing. The fish is still part of the school, and for a moment it seems as if I have hooked the whole lot of them out there as they boil and circle the inlet's mouth. Finally I gain a measure of control and isolate my quarry in the shallows behind my casting platform. The fish is a male developing the first suggestions of the kype with which it will soon be tending its redd somewhere upstream. I reach down, flick the streamer from its lip, and let both of us get on with our business.

As I straighten from the water, I realize that everyone else has stopped fishing. In fact, all the tourists are staring at me with faintly amazed expressions. I remember that they have been fishing unsuccessfully for red salmon all morning, and that this fish fell to the very first cast I made in their presence. The honorable thing to do would be to confess, to admit that I have been casting to these same fish all morning without a strike, to tell them that this apparently brilliant moment of success was above all else the product of dumb luck. But then I have never been a particularly honorable sort of guy.

"How did you *do* that?" one of their number finally calls across the water.

"Practice!" I shout back. At least there is a degree of honesty in this admission.

"Reds," the charter pilot repeats in dismay as I slog back past him toward the Cub. We both know that his customers will expect him to tell them what to do now, even though fishing is not supposed to be his job, or his problem. I stop and offer him a handful of red-salmon flies, which he accepts gratefully. Someone will have to figure out how to deliver them to the fish with spinning tackle, but that someone will not be me. I've made my peace with the guide business once again.

Back at my own airplane, I break the rod down and store it in the metal tube fixed behind the rear seat for just this purpose. One is enough today; I have no more business with the red salmon. Set free from the beach at last, the Cub drifts away from the shore, and when it pivots naturally into the wind I let it sail backward down the lake so no one will be blasted with prop wash when the engine starts. Such simple courtesies are usually noted only in their absence. The tourists have converged around the Cessna and I can see them inspecting the selection of flies intently. I hope they figure out some way to cast them. I even hope they catch some fish if that's what it takes for them to enjoy their day and for my friend to enjoy his.

Reds. . . . Give them long enough and they'll make philosophers of us all.

SEVENTEEN

THE TWENTY-MINUTE RULE

Tarpon: *Megalops atlantica*

I REMEMBER MY FIRST TARPON about as vividly as I remember anything. In fact, I remember it more clearly than I remember a number of other things that are supposed to count as seminal events in a man's life, which may be more of an admission about my priorities than I really ought to be making.

Even when you're having fun there, the mangrove-studded flats between the barrier islands of Belize and the mainland should remind you just how inhospitable the tropical marine environment can be. A real-life shipwreck survivor would have one tough time if he or she washed up on those shores. The comfortable sand beaches that dominate our images of the tropics turn out to be few and far between, and anyone looking for potable water might as well be in the middle of the Sahara. Of all the tundra, swamp, muskeg, and other nasty stuff there is to walk on in the outdoors, nothing is quite as impossible as the marl that forms the bottom of the barrier islands' leeward flats, which means that those who venture there will be confined to boats for most of their stay. The sun overhead can be relentless, and should the breeze falter, hordes of biting insects will be waiting to make the visitor's acquaintance.

I can remember when Belize was about as far off the beaten path as you could get. There was no tourist presence to speak of then, and the crowds of American divers, eco-adventurers, and aging hippies that now jam the airport in Belize City had yet to materialize. Things were certainly simpler then, and when you had done what you had to do to get yourself out onto those lonely, spooky, wonderful, never-ending flats, you could almost imagine that you and the other occupants of your boat were either the first or the last people on earth, although it was occasionally less than clear whether this distinction should count as reward or punishment.

It was Sheli and Armando and I that day. We started out catching bonefish back in the mangrove creeks, but the fish were all small; when the wind fell away, the heat and the bugs near shore became unbearable, so we rode the tide down the channel and dropped the motor and ran. We told ourselves that we were going tarpon fishing, but what we were really doing was getting away from the stifling heat and the sand flies.

It was early in the season for tarpon on the flats according to both Armando and everything I knew, but we lost the bugs on the run across the open water, and by the time we cut the motor and began to drift I was starting to feel like a survivor. We stopped upwind from one of Armando's secret mackerel holes and caught a few fish for dinner, and then we rigged up for tarpon.

Saying that we rigged up for tarpon is something of an exaggeration. I didn't own any really heavy saltwater tackle then. I was using the same 8-weight rod I used for bonefish and salmon, and the reel was one of those simple affairs with a useless excuse for a drag that is basically little more than a repository for line. That was about all the muscle I had the money or the inclination for back then. I had learned to palm the reel adroitly enough to manage most fish in the light saltwater class, but I had never asked it to do anything remotely like what I was about to ask it to do that day. And so in the final analysis, rigging for tarpon amounted to little more than tying a length of shock tippet to the end of my leader with an Albright Special, attaching a gaudy orange streamer to the end of the shock tippet, hitting the hook with a few strokes from my file, and hoping for the best.

The breeze had freshened and Sheli was worried about casting the heavy streamer in the wind, so I climbed up onto the bow of the skiff. Actually, Sheli was every bit as capable of doing the casting as I was; she was just less immune to embarrassment. Then Armando began to pole, and Sheli settled into a book and a bite of lunch while I stood and braced myself against the slap of the waves on the boat's chine and studied the water ahead for fish.

You were introduced to the mysterious visual challenge of sight-fishing ocean flats in an earlier chapter. Suffice it to say that nowhere are the deceptive qualities of tropical sun on water more apparent than they are on open, expansive flats like these, where there is little or no sense of horizon and nothing to define the figure-ground relationships that keep us from going crazy whenever we open our eyes. Factor in the hypnotic rhythm of the water against the skiff and it's easy to imagine how an uninterrupted morning of this kind of thing can make you feel like the veteran of a sensory deprivation experiment.

I really don't know how long we were at it before the fish appeared, but suddenly they were there at eleven o'clock off the bow, a pod of dark-green shapes that could only have been tarpon or saltwater crocodiles. "Sabalo!" Armando hissed from the stern as I tried to false cast without worrying too much about what would happen if the lethal orange monster on the end of the shock tippet hit one of us in the crosswind.

We had closed right down on top of the fish by now, and I could see their huge, cold eyes and the ragged geometry of their silver scales when I finally cast. The streamer hit the water well in front of the leading fish. As I began to retrieve the fly, I looked down to see an impossible bird's nest in the line lying on the skiff's bow. To hook the tarpon at this point would be not only to lose the fish but to lose the rod and reel as well.

"Strip!" Armando shouted from the stern.

"I can't!" I shouted back as I let the fly sink lifelessly in front of the tarpon and started to pick my way through the mess underfoot. The last fish had cruised past by the time the final loop fell free. Armando strained to bring the skiff about as I made a second desperate cast. The fly landed awkwardly in the middle of the school and the tarpon fluttered at the disturbance like nervous birds. And when I began to strip the streamer back toward the boat, one of them peeled away from the pack and began to track the fly like a dog intent on a running pheasant.

Nothing can really prepare you for the visual excitement of a tarpon's strike. A tarpon's jaw angles sharply upward from its corner toward the incisors so that its mouth seems to open right on top of its head. When my fish finally darted beneath the streamer, I could peer right down into its gullet as it struck. Then it inhaled the fly with a noise that sounded like a toilet flushing. I hit the fish as hard as I thought the rod could stand, and all the morning's easy tranquillity disappeared forever.

Few of us are accustomed to finding ourselves face to face with gamefish near our own size, but at the sting of the hook, the tarpon exploded from the water right in front of the skiff's bow and there we were, me and my personal Moby Dick. The fish looked cold and primitive and beautiful all at once as it hung there in the air with its red gills flaring and its huge plated scales alive with the brilliance of the morning sun. I knew I should be concentrating on getting the free line started smoothly through the lowest guide, but I could not take my eyes away from this fish as it crashed back into the sea and then rose and fell again and again.

The rest of the tarpon were still out there charging about like overgrown baitfish under the influence of amphetamines. After a fast, hard series of jumps, my fish rejoined the school and the bunch of them took off for the horizon together. Somehow, the coils of line lying at my feet organized themselves into something capable of finding its way through a fly rod's guides, and I was playing the fish from the reel at last.

This is generally acknowledged to be a critical juncture in the battle with a tarpon on the fly, the moment at which things can reasonably be expected to go right, at least for a while. This expectation, however, presumes a reel that is up to the task, one that at least boasts a functional drag other than the heel of your hand. As a longtime advocate of light tackle in the pursuit of everything from fish to grizzly bears to life itself, it has been my position that you can always hook one (or shoot one, or whatever) and then worry about what you've gotten yourself into later. Well there I was, hooked up big as life to a fish capable of turning me and my equipment into toast. It was time to start worrying.

There is often strength in numbers for fish as well as for people. Emboldened by its companions, the tarpon ran with the school for deep water, and it took well over a hundred yards of pressure to break the fish out of the pack. It did not jump after it began that first sustained run. In fact, it would not jump again, and if I had known that, or had an accurate sense of what was to come, I might simply have clamped my hand down on the reel face and been done with the whole business. But no. Not me.

The fact was, I had suddenly gotten caught up in a whole lot of *The Old Man and the Sea* mental bullshit, and for the first time in years it felt singularly important that I land this particular fish. It was my first tarpon, and that was part of it, but above and beyond this fact I think I recognized an opportunity to do something ridiculous and therefore paradoxically grand. Land a tarpon on a trout rod. Come on.

And because it had become important that I land the fish and count coup, I fought it as if all this mattered, which is to say grimly and without regard for enjoyment. The fish began to bore its way around the nearest cay with relentless determination, while I hung on and Armando poled leisurely from the stern and Sheli quite reasonably dug herself something cold out of the ice chest. In our own ways, we were each settling in for a war of attrition.

Smoking reels must rank among the most odious clichés in outdoor writing, but I soon realized that something dramatic had happened to mine. It was hot and it wobbled as it revolved like a wheel about to part company from an axle. In fact, the force of the tarpon's first run had essentially blown out its guts, leaving me to handle the fish with tackle that was functionally indistinguishable from the gear I used to subdue perch when I was five years old.

The first trip around the cay took over an hour. Armando settled into his *Que sera, sera* mode while Sheli worked on her tan. I imply no criticism; there was nothing else for either of them to do. I tried to horse the fish a time or two, but whenever I did, the tarpon did something to remind me of the David and Goliath aspects of the situation and I backed right off.

By the time we were halfway around the cay the second time, even I couldn't stand it anymore. I pumped and reeled with abandon until I had the smooth, familiar feel of the fly line in my hand again. Finally the exhausted fish was wallowing next to the boat, Armando flicked the gaff through its lip, and everyone collapsed together in the middle of the skiff with an odd mixture of triumph and relief as the tarpon lay panting next to the gunwale.

Against considerable odds, I had caught a tarpon on a fly, but there were still decisions to be made. None of the usual options (release it, photograph it, kill it) seemed appropriate, so I just jumped over the side of the boat and grabbed it. As soon as I did, all sorts of illusions began to unravel. Jumping and running, it had been the Silver King of legend, but now it lay inert and defeated. Sure it was big, but its apparent size as it hung suspended in the sun was deceptive, for the fish was thin through the middle like a deer at the end of a long winter. The mouth felt hard as metal inside, and the 3/0 hook had scarcely nicked it. As I cradled the fish in my arms and struggled to stay upright in the marl, I studied the goofy angle of the tarpon's jaw and stared into its cold, stupid eye, unable to suppress the thought that when all was said and done, I had just spent two and a half hours landing a hundred-pound kipper.

Tarpon are one of those species whose whole somehow seems more than the sum of its parts. They keep showing up on short lists of the world's greatest gamefish. A number of our better-known saltwater fly-rod authorities seem to have made their reputations on tarpon, even though there are more challenging quarries in the sea. And then there is the business of the benchmark two-hundred-pounder. The thought of being the first to catch one on a fly seems to affect a lot of dedicated anglers the way the possibility of a four-minute mile used to affect middle-distance runners. All this adds up to either mystique or hype, depending on whether you approach the outdoor world from the romantic or the cynical point of view.

There is certainly nothing wrong with any of this, although I personally approach certain aspects of the tarpon's reputation with detachment. In the field, I'm quite willing to pass up numerous opportunities at game animals that most people would be happy to harvest, just for the chance to keep hunting for something exceptional. It seems that if the same instincts were ever to prevail with the fly rod, it should be the tarpon that excites them, what with their size and the flavor of the epic that surrounds their taking. If I care so much about big elk and big whitetails, why don't I care about big tarpon? I don't know. Once you're out of the baby tarpon class—the little ten- to fifteen-pounders that you catch in out-of-the-way lagoons—all tarpon seem pretty much the same to me. I've never weighed one in my life. Other people can worry about being the first to catch a two-hundred-pound tarpon on a fly. Leave me out of the loop, thank you.

In the first place, I'll never fish with tackle heavy enough to land one. In the second place, I don't go fishing in order to worry.

Back in town the night after our marathon struggle, we learned that Ray had also landed a tarpon after a protracted battle on light fly tackle, which provided an excuse for much celebration over beer and conch fritters. At first, I chose not to share with anyone my deconstructed image of the Silver King as overgrown baitfish. It fell to Sheli to allow reality to intrude on the euphoria of the moment.

"The thing is," she finally said, "watching someone land a tarpon is just plain boring. I mean, an hour is one thing, but that was ridiculous."

"It was," I admitted with relief. "Just standing there, applying pressure. Well that's just fine, but pressure works both ways."

"That was two hours we could have been bonefishing," Sheli pointed out.

"The take," Ray remembered wistfully. "The insane jumping and the first wild run. Then it all got to be work."

Obviously, we had come away from this experience with remarkably similar impressions of what had met our expectations and what had not. Since we planned to do a lot more tarpon fishing in our lives, beginning early the following morning, all that remained was to codify these observations into a plan that would save as much of the magic as possible and allow us to discard the rest. It was Ray who first pointed out how front-loaded the experience of hooking a tarpon was, at least on a temporal scale. All the good stuff came right at the beginning: the huge fish sucking the fly down into its maw and running and jumping and shimmying as if nature had hired a stripper just for you. The rest of it we could do without.

And so we called for another round of Charger and formulated the Twenty-Minute Rule, a private bit of legislation as remarkable for its brevity as for its effectiveness. Since there would almost always be two of us in the skiff while we were tarpon fishing, we agreed that at the moment of the strike, the second party would glance at his or her watch, and by the time twenty minutes had elapsed, the tarpon would either be boated or broken off.

It was simple in theory and it proved simple in practice as well. The next morning, Ray was up in the bow when the tarpon appeared. After the usual fumbling he managed an accurate cast, and then the hooked fish was shaking its plated sides at us in the sun. I glanced at my watch and reached for my camera as Ray struck the fish a second time, and then there was nothing to do but hang on and let the tarpon happen to us as it leaped and ran.

The real excitement didn't last all that long, however, and by the time fifteen minutes had passed Ray was looking less like an angler than someone working out in a gym. Despite applying pressure with careless abandon, he was still well down in his backing when I finally bellowed, "Time!"

"No problem," he replied with obvious relief, and then he clamped his hand down on the reel and lowered the rod tip, and when the leader snapped we all felt as free as the fish. "You're up," Ray said as he climbed down from the bow. "Let's go find some more tarpon."

And that's just what we did.

Several years later, I was snorkeling the reef somewhere in the Turneffe Islands when I drifted out over the edge of the blue water and found myself right in the middle of a school of tarpon. This was an utterly new perspective, and one that few anglers will ever share. Viewed in their own element, they were bright and powerful, and I think that if I had seen them like that at first, I might never have concluded that landing one on a fly was something to be done as expeditiously as possible. It was too late to revoke the Twenty-Minute Rule by then, however, and it remains part of our tribal law as certainly as if it came to us from Moses engraved in stone instead of from a table covered with empty beer bottles.

I've often wondered why catching big fish (and weighing and measuring and photographing them, and all that other stuff) doesn't appeal to me more. I'm the kind of guy who *ought* to be excited by the idea of taking a two-hundred-pound tarpon on a fly, but I'm not. As a matter of fact, it wouldn't bother me if I never caught another tarpon in my life.

But tarpon fishing, as opposed to tarpon catching, is another matter. To spot the fish, to cast to them, to watch one break away from the pack and charge the fly and open that great, gaping mouth . . . therein lies the object of the game. Others can worry about how much the fish weighs, about where to put it when it returns from the taxidermist, about their place in history.

I'd rather give it twenty minutes and then go look for another fish.

EIGHTEEN

LOVELY, DARK, AND DEEP

Arctic Char: *Salvelinus alpinus*
Far Eastern Char: *Salvelinus leucomaenis*
Lake Trout: *Salvelinus namaycush*

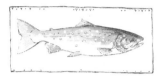

I FEEL SORRY FOR CHAR. As a genus, they seem destined to live out their lives in the trout's shadow for reasons that are difficult to articulate, but which certainly go beyond the distribution of teeth along the vomer, which is how biologists, as opposed to fools with fly rods, tell the two apart.

Few would argue with the inclusion of the brook trout in a short list of our continent's heavy hitters on the fly, even though it is not a trout at all, a fact that I refused to accept for the first decade of my life until my father, always the stickler for scientific precision, showed me the brutal truth in a book. Even so, the brook trout probably owes as much of its reputation to geographical coincidence as to its innate qualities as a gamefish. Being pretty never hurts the cause either.

Of course, we have already been through two chapters' worth of char. Conventional wisdom would suggest that this is enough slumming, and that we ought to get on with things and return to the glamour species, to which course of action I would raise two objections: In the first place, we're about out of glamour species. In the second place, and more to the point, I happen to like char for a variety of reasons, both honorable and suspect: They tend to inhabit wild, lonely places; they are beautiful; they taste good; and they often aren't very bright.

Promoting all of these qualities as virtues certainly could make *me* suspect in the minds of many purists, but we have probably parted company from the stuffiest of them by now anyway. In the end, it bothers me not one bit to admit that I often feel something like a char myself, except for the part about being beautiful and good to eat.

Here are brief notes on three more members of the genus *Salvelinus*.

It is mid-August, although right now anyone used to enjoying late summer in shirt sleeves and shorts might have trouble placing themselves on that page of the calendar. The sun is shining low on the southern horizon, and all around us snow is yielding to its glare. Behind camp, the Brooks Range rolls up and away like an abstract sculpture made of whipped cream, while downriver the Arctic Ocean waits, a cold, gray snake insinuating its way between the offshore ice pack and the weathered headlands of the coast. It is difficult to imagine any place else on earth more totally dedicated to the proposition of loneliness.

I am cold and tired and wet and hungry, all in no particular order. We flew in a week earlier in search of sheep the color of the snow, but the blizzard drove us back down out of the mountains and very nearly out of our minds after spending three days huddled in a backpack tent doing nothing more ambitious than trying to stay alive. At least we accomplished that, and as hunts go this one will have to be accounted not by the length of the rams' horns but by the fact of our survival.

I couldn't afford the luxury of carrying fishing gear into the mountains because of weight considerations, but here at the makeshift gravel-bar airstrip I have a fly rod stashed with an extra duffel bag full of survival gear. During the long confinement in the tent, it was difficult not to think about the fish we had seen in the river earlier. When we landed, the pool beside the river had been full of arctic char in the five- to seven-pound range. The water ran impossibly clear, and the fish hung suspended in the pool like brilliant bits of fruit in gelatin salad. The vivid orange and pink markings on their sides had been impossible to forget as the world faded to black and white around us, and now I needed to see them again the way you sometimes need to see old friends.

The arctic char is something of a misfit even by the less-than-

---

dignified standards of its genus. Some authorities regard it as co-specific with the Dolly Varden, and given the recent advances in our technical ability to settle such debates once and for all in the laboratory, it's probably only a matter of time until some well-meaning nerd camped out in a room full of computers does just that. The two fish are certainly similar in appearance, although Dollies tend to have smaller spots than do arctic char. I've never worried about this very much, since the two seem distinct the way brown and grizzly bears seem distinct in spite of the biologists' insistence that they are one and the same, as they no doubt are genetically.

Whatever the arctic char's shortcomings, and there are many, no one can reasonably deny that they are among our most handsome gamefish. It is their beauty that I really need from them now rather than their potential for sport or food, although I am hardly oblivious to the latter possibilities. After the long, exhausting hike and the frustration of the hunt that did not come to pass and the mountains' cold rebuke of our intrusion, I need to be reassured that nature can reward as well as censure, and I cannot imagine a better means of doing so than by addressing a pool full of fish with a fly rod.

Once our camp is secure, I dig the pack rod and my wilderness belly bag out of the duffel and walk down to the river. There are fresh grizzly tracks in the sand, but the bears and I have made our peace on this trip and I don't give them a second thought. The river has risen with the melting snow, and the newly colored current hides its own secrets as I climb onto a boulder and begin to work out line. I cannot see the bottom and I cannot see the fish, but I know they are there, able to run but finally unable to hide.

I cast and lift and cast again. Not much happens for some time. A herd of caribou appears on the barren horizon, and with my bow-hunting instincts aroused from dormancy, I stop and glass them, but they're all cows and youngsters. Then somewhere out in the water the streamer hesitates. I strike and find myself fast to a fish.

Let's face it: Char don't qualify as members of the upper echelons of gamefish according to their fighting ability. A brilliantly colored fish, this one looks to be in the six- or seven-pound range when it finally rolls to the surface. A rainbow or brown in that weight class would have me running up and down the bank in a frenzy calling for nets and cameras and witnesses, but despite its size, my char just can't bother getting too excited about the presence of the hook in its lip, and consequently, neither can I.

By the time I vector the fish out of the water and onto the gravel bar with steady pressure from the little pack rod, my thoughts have turned to a pressing if politically incorrect subject: dinner. For better or worse, one arena in which char consistently bring the competition to its knees is the serving platter. All char taste good, and specimens like this one can excite the palate like nothing else from fresh water. It has been a long week of boiled noodles and freeze-dried horse fodder, and as I bend over the panting fish, predatory instincts rise ominously inside my heart.

The trouble is that the fish is just so beautiful. You would ordinarily have to go to a tropical reef to find colors like these on something that swims, and even then they would be different somehow, rendered imprecise by their own gaudy company. Here, there is nothing but snow and ice and rock in the background, against which the char stands out like a collection of crown jewels. This is stupid, I tell myself firmly. This is hopelessly sentimental. We are hungry.

Oh, hell. I release the fish.

This recounting must end on a note of mystery. Perhaps I caught another fish from the pool and carried it back to camp to cook in chunks over my butane stove, and perhaps I just reeled in and called it a day. There were certainly good arguments to be made for either course of action. The historical truth of the matter remains north of the Arctic Circle, which seems to be a perfectly good place for it. The fact remains that it takes a lot of beauty to stay the hand of the beast.

Remember that the next time someone speaks disparagingly about char in contrast to the established glamour species.

"Kundzha," Sergei announced gravely as he pointed toward the riffle.

"Got it," I replied.

In fact, I did not have it at all. After three weeks in the Russian bush, I wasn't sure I had much of anything except sore feet and an abiding respect for everything and everyone who managed to survive there. We were exploring and bowhunting grizzly bears, and it was hard to be sure which activity was more irrational. At least we had taken our fishing gear. Thank God for that.

The rivers were full of dog salmon and the bears were right there feeding on them, all of which was either good news or bad news depending on one's attitude toward dog salmon and grizzly bears. We had already learned that being within bow range of the grizzlies was something you could only take so much of without a break, and our fly rods and the fish-choked rivers had been providing just the right excuse for some badly needed midday R&R. After several days of this, however, I wasn't sure I could stand any more dog salmon. Over lunch, I explained my need for some variety as best I could, and an hour later I was standing next to a clear-water tributary with Sergei.

I still had no idea what a *kundzha* was, but Sergei seemed certain they were out there and worthy of our attention. So I rigged up, tied a generic streamer to the leader, and began to fish. Nothing exciting happened on the first dozen casts, which was frankly all right with me, since we had spent an eventful morning with the bears and I didn't really need any excitement for a while. Then Sergei began to pace and fidget until it was no longer possible to ignore him. There followed one of our long, inconclusive efforts at Soviet-American communications that consisted for the most part of lots of pantomime while we exhausted the possibilities of our limited mutual vocabulary.

Finally we settled on the word *caviar*. We had eaten plenty of the fresh red variety in camp courtesy of the dog salmon, but it wasn't time for lunch and I had no idea what Sergei was talking about until he seized the streamer distastefully and dismissed it with a chorus of nyets. Finally lights started going on in my brain, and when I produced a single-egg pattern from my fly book the smile on Sergei's face told me that we had reached an understanding. Perhaps our common survival of the Cold War was not the accident it sometimes seems.

On its maiden voyage through the riffle, the egg fly managed to do just what the streamer had not, which was to induce an immediate strike from something that was too vigorous and quick to be another dog salmon. In fact, it was so vigorous and quick that I missed the strike completely, to Sergei's obvious dismay. *"Kundzha,"* he sighed wistfully as I slogged up toward the top end of the run with my curiosity thoroughly aroused.

I mishandled several more pickups at the head of the riffle. The takes were as subtle as those of nymphing spring-creek browns, and by the time I realized what I was dealing with, Sergei was insisting that we head back to camp for lunch. As we hiked downriver, my only regret was that the elusive *kundzha* still remained a mystery.

Back in camp, however, I found Ray studying a fish that Sergei immediately and happily identified as none other than a *kundzha*. Weighing in at around three pounds, Ray's specimen was an intriguing, bullet-nosed char with dark, colorless sides adorned with creamy white spots, all of which gave it at least a passing resemblance to our North American lake trout. Ray confirmed its affinity for egg patterns and its crafty approach to the fly, and he also volunteered that it was one hot number when hooked.

At the time, we knew nothing more about the *kundzha* except that the Russians very much wanted Ray's fish in the soup pot, which was scarcely a culinary discriminator since the same pot had already produced meals made from salmon heads and grizzly paws and virtually anything else that might suggest a source of protein in the lean and hungry Russian bush. Later, after our return home, I would learn that the proper Anglicized common name for the species is the Far Eastern char, although it has also been called the white-spotted char in older fisheries literature. I also learned that nobody really seemed to know much more about the species than we did, which meant that I had become something of an expert on the Far Eastern char by simple virtue of having seen one. The Russians claimed that *kundzha* grow big and fight hard, all of which certainly sounds intriguing—enough so, in fact, that a return trip to the waters that hold them is still on my wish list of future expeditions.

In the meanwhile, I like to imagine another small marvel that might yet accrue from the end of the Cold War: the discovery of a mysterious char with the potential to earn its entire genus new respect as gamefish.

When I was a young kid growing up in northern New York, we didn't get to fish for much of anything big. Brook trout were our staple quarry, and a twelve-incher was the kind of trophy you dragged around to display to all your friends. There were some pickerel and bass, but they weren't very big either. Once or twice each summer my friends and I would go down to the river with worms and dough balls and try to catch carp, which were at least large enough to give us a taste of what it might be like to have a substantial fish on the end of a line. Even the carp were enough to let me know that big fish were worth pursuing, although at the time I had no idea quite where this discovery would eventually lead me.

We lived next to a deep lake rumored to hold lake trout, which enjoyed a local reputation similar to that of the *yeti*. There were people who were said to know people who had seen them, but that was about as far as it went. People certainly did go out and troll for them on long, calm summer evenings, but from my perspective on the dock, those adventures seemed little more than excuses to enjoy the company of other men's wives. At the age of ten, I was way too serious an angler to be interested in wasting time like that.

One of the most dedicated lake-trout anglers in town was a friend of my father's whom I worshipped because he was always happy to take me fishing on those occasions when my father could not do so himself. My mother was not altogether happy with his influence, since (as I learned later) he was locally renowned not only for his skill as a fisherman but for his ability to raise hell as well. It never came to an ultimatum, however, probably because my mother found him so useful when it came to getting me out of the house on days when I was driving her crazy with requests that someone take me fishing.

One evening he arrived in his station wagon and called us all down from the porch to examine the contents of his ice chest. He was as excited as I had ever seen him, and I knew that for once there would be something in the cooler besides empty cans. We all walked down the steps together and he threw the ice chest lid open as if he could not quite believe its contents himself, and there it was, close to twenty pounds' worth of lake trout, as intimidating a slab of fish as I had ever seen.

After this flash of inspiration, we all did a lot of lake-trout fishing for a while. This consisted of trolling large plugs around the lake with lead-core line and heavy tackle perfectly suitable for saltwater bottom-fishing. It didn't take me long to learn that I didn't like lake-trout fishing much in spite of the vivid memory of that huge, marvelous fish resting in the bottom of the ice chest. Simply put, it was more fun catching six-inch brook trout on fly rods, although I'm not sure that my newfound sense of purism would have withstood the taking of even one good-size lake trout.

And there the matter of lake trout might have rested had it not been for a wilderness canoe trip in Ontario a year or so later.

It was late May, not long after ice-out, and we were half a dozen portages beyond the nearest road. Late in the afternoon of the third or fourth day, we were paddling along the edge of a lake looking for a suitable place to camp. Actually, my father was paddling; I was in the bow casting a streamer in toward shore. I had caught several pan-size brook trout, and since the afternoon was clear and beautiful and the black-flies hadn't found us, it was hard to imagine that things could be any better—and then, suddenly, they were.

The fly, as I remember distinctly, was a Gray Ghost, a lovely and perfectly useful pattern that makes me regret that no one pays much attention to classic streamer patterns anymore. They were fun to tie and fun to fish, especially when they went down hard and solid in the maw of something substantial the way this one did. For a moment we thought I might have hooked a world-record brook trout, but finally I worked the fish up next to the canoe and we saw that it wasn't quite that big and that it wasn't a brook trout either. Those gray flanks, those creamy spots. . . . To our amazement, we had taken a lake trout on a fly.

The fish looked to be a five-pounder or thereabouts, not large by lake-trout standards, but plenty of fish to me, especially on the tackle I was using. It dawned on us that something unusual was happening, and that vast possibilities lay beneath the slick, black water. My father cleared his throat and announced that this was a great time for me to work on my stern-paddling technique, so we traded places and he took up the fly rod, and within a matter of minutes we had done it again. We caught several more lakers on the same fly before the lengthening shadows told us that it was time to stop playing and set up camp. May would never be quite the same for us again.

There must be proper scientific explanations for the fleeting phenomenon of lake trout at the surface early in the year, no doubt involving thermal gradients and similar mysteries familiar to those who fish still waters regularly and well. Having no sophisticated knowledge of the subject, we just guessed. For the next several years, until my family moved to the Pacific Northwest, we regularly canoed into the same lake system during late May, but we caught the lake trout on the surface only once again.

If I were ever to live in serious lake-trout country, I suspect I might make a science of catching lake trout on the fly. That has never come to pass. There are lake trout in Montana, but there are just too many other things to pursue. Alaska actually has some good lake-trout fishing, but the species' principal appeal—size—doesn't mean all that much in a land of anadromous giants.

Even if I never catch another lake trout, I'll be content with the memory of the evening when a remote lake opened up its heart to reveal itself to me the way a lover might share some intimate secret.

Now we have examined together every char I know. Comparing them to trout and salmon is to compare apples to oranges. The fact that arctic char are not rainbow trout should not be held against either species. A proper enjoyment of the outdoor world depends on appreciating differences, and this is simply another one to be appreciated.

By virtue of geography and habit, most fly-fishers will never know the subjects of this chapter. This is a pity, as all three live in places worth visiting. In the meanwhile, keep an open mind. Who knows? Perhaps the *kundzha* will become the next glamour species.

If so, remember where you heard it first.

NINETEEN

GONE TO THE DOGS

Chum Salmon: *Oncorhynchus keta*

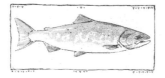

DATELINE: EASTERN SIBERIA. We are standing on the shore of the river that provided the region's early ethnic Russian explorers with their first route to the Pacific, just as the Columbia led Lewis and Clark to the opposite side of the same body of water. This river is an order of magnitude smaller, however. In fact, by choosing our route carefully, we can cross it in hip waders. Portland sits at the mouth of the Columbia; the mouth of this tumbling stream is occupied by the same bears and seabirds that lived here two centuries earlier, and by very little else. Somewhere in the divergent histories of these two waterways to the sea lies a measure of progress, but I'm not quite sure how to frame it.

The same weather patterns that generate Alaska's notoriously evil climate keep the bad stuff spinning thataway out of the Bering Sea. Consequently, the North Pacific's far eastern coast remains surprisingly dry, and for going on two weeks we have enjoyed calm, blue skies overhead. The current is running as clear as the vodka that is ever present around the campfire at night, as we pursue our personal diplomatic mission of forging an end to the Cold War. The river is colder than the vodka, which the Russians insist we belt down straight right along with them. It also contains more fish, although by the second or third bottle, the vodka usually manages some valiant competition. Now, after a

161

long day of hiking through the alpine above camp, I am ready for the river and its contents.

Back in camp at last, I exchange longbow for fly rod and set off in search of something to catch. My friend Doug Borland is an hour or so ahead of me, and I follow his bootprints through the bear tracks in the sand for a mile or so downstream until I spot him on a gravel bar casting with grim determination. "The river is full of *keta*," he announces as I join him and survey the water. "But they won't hit anything."

As a linguistic aside, the Russian common name for all Pacific salmon species is the same as the specific half of their scientific name. Hence, *Oncorhynchus keta* in fisheries bulletins becomes just plain *keta* in the Russian bush. Visiting fly-fishers should bone up on this terminology before they go, since communications there are never easy and we would all prefer to spend our time with the *kisutch* rather than the *gorbuscha*.

But here stands Doug, who knows all this perfectly well, and who still wears the look of a man for whom the fishing is not living up to expectations. One hard look down into the current explains those expectations clearly. The river is teeming with dog salmon, whose variegate green and maroon flanks make them the easiest of the salmon species to identify in fresh water. While their calico markings may win few points in the cult of the mint-bright salmon (in which I cheerfully confess membership), sometimes rational values must prevail. These fish are fresh from the nearby sea, and most look to be pushing twenty pounds. Clearly it is time to catch some.

I watch Doug cast again as I run my leader through the guides. He is a tall man with plenty of power in his casting arm, and now he is sending his fly whistling far out across the water with the go-to-hell attitude of someone who has been casting to lots of anadromous fish for too long without a strike. "What have you been using?" I inquire helpfully.

"Every ridiculous fly I own," he replies, sounding like someone who has passed beyond science and into the realm of desperation.

"Perhaps you should consider using a dog-salmon fly."

Doug and I have shared difficult times from one end of the outdoor world to the other without exchanging a harsh word, but now he turns and fixes me with a hard stare that lets me know I'm on thin ice. "There is no such thing," he replies. "These are dog salmon, not spring-creek browns. They're gonna hit or they aren't."

"Whatever you say," I reply slyly, as I rummage through my belly bag and close my fingers first on the battered leather fly book that has served as my wilderness emergency fishing kit from one end of the Pacific Rim to the other, and then finally on the fly itself. A minute later, I've got the thing on the end of the leader and then in the air and then in the water and then smack into a fish, which proceeds to thrash and roll and otherwise carry on right in front of Doug until I'm almost embarrassed. But not quite.

As fighters, dogs fall around the middle of the Pacific salmon pack, but when they're as fresh and large as this one, they can give anyone a workout on light fly tackle. Finally I ease the fish into the shallows and slide the hook from its snaggletoothed, menacing jaw. "Luck," Doug sniffs from his position farther up the gravel bar.

"Right," I reply merrily, and then two casts later I'm fast to another fish. Doug flails the water intently while I repeat the process of landing and releasing my quarry. But when I tag a third dog moments later, he can stand it no longer.

"What do you call that thing?" he asks, studying the flashy green streamer left behind as I release my latest fish and watch it slide back to freedom in the current.

"Never got around to giving it a name," I admit.

"You wouldn't happen to have an extra lying around, would you?" Doug asks in a voice that could sponsor a charity.

"Indeed I do," I respond, after a melodramatic inspection of my fly book. "Of course, the price on specialty items goes up out here in the bush."

"How much?" Doug asks, and it's clear from the tone of his voice that he's resigned to his fate.

I study the clear sky overhead, searching abstractly for a measure of the streamer's value. "A thousand dollars," I finally announce. Doug casts his fly into the river. I cast my fly into the river. I hook another fish. This is becoming painful. "Or," I suggest with tact worthy of a diplomat, "a beer."

Doug has been appointed guardian of the case of Carlsberg we smuggled aboard the helicopter that dumped us off beside the river, and he has since meted out its contents according to a draconian rationing schedule. Silently he gauges the heat and the enormity of his thirst while I play the last salmon to a standstill. When I straighten again after releasing the fish, he is standing with his hand extended like a beggar. I mumble some nonsense about parting with family heirlooms as I hand him the last of my green streamers, but the salesmanship is overkill. Everyone knows who's been had, and that some of the countless hours I've squandered at the fly-tying bench have finally been justified.

It goes without saying that you don't become an expert at catching dog salmon on a fly by accident. Dogs (or chums, or whatever you want to call them) never seem to draw a lot of fire even among experienced Pacific salmon anglers, especially those who insist on going about it with fly tackle. Acquiring real proficiency requires spending several days camped beside an airplane waiting for the weather to lift so that you can go somewhere, anywhere. At first you break out the gear you have packed around in the rod tube all summer and cast something at the dogs because it's fun. Then you cast at them because there's nothing else to do. Finally, you touch up your hooks and check your leader and fish for them as if you mean business, because you've run out of canned stew and there's nothing else to eat. That's when you remember that no one fishes—really fishes—quite like a hungry fisherman. When you finally get off that gravel bar and a few more like it, you will know all about dog salmon and fly rods. Believe me.

The dog may be the most difficult of the Pacific salmon species to read from the sporting perspective. While they look downright inviting in salt water, where sport anglers almost never see them, the characteristic spawning colors they acquire almost immediately upon reaching the streams are, at the least, an aesthetic liability among bright-salmon enthusiasts.

Then there is their name. I mean, who wants to fish for *dogs?* Commercial-fishing interests have tried to soften this image by calling them chums, at least in public, although you'll never hear the term aboard a drift boat. Some Alaska sport anglers make a point of calling them calico salmon, a term that is at least vaguely descriptive, even though no one will know what you are talking about should you use it. Perhaps the Russo-scientific *keta* deserves a more prominent place on this list of euphemisms. I rather like it myself.

But dogs they are, even though opinions differ as to how they earned their name. Is it because they look like dogs? Taste like dogs? Make good sled-dog food? Spending time on one of the little tributaries where *keta* spawn should clarify this question definitively. All Pacific salmon develop fierce, exaggerated features prior to spawning, which primarily serve the cosmetic functions of threat display. Not so the *keta,* whose disposition on the spawning grounds is every bit as ferocious as its appearance. Males develop truly impressive teeth (from which removing an embedded hook requires due caution) and guard their redds savagely. When a neighboring male wanders too close, the offended party will predictably rip into the intruder just like, well, a dog.

For the fly-fisher intent on catching them, these aggressive characteristics translate into the potential for lots of action, especially since these traits are not confined to the spawning grounds, where no one should be fishing for salmon in the first place. Dogs in fresh water are less likely to disappoint by way of sullen mood than most other Pacific salmon species. Factor in their size (second only to the king) and their numbers and you have a quarry worthy of attention.

While fly selection for dog salmon is not to be confused with rocket science, I have consistently done better with the pattern I used that afternoon in Russia than with any other randomly selected bright streamer. In fact, the fly is effective on all salmon, which is why after some thought I eventually christened it the GAFF, or Generic Anadromous Fish Fly. (Note that I waited until the last chapter to offer any concrete advice from the tying bench. I promised this would not be a how-to book.) The GAFF consists of a white bucktail underwing and silver body topped by blue Flashabou and green bucktail, all served up on a long-shank hook. I believe that it imitates the small Dollies that harass spawning salmon on the redds, which is why it incites such an aggressive and transspecific response. It's a theory, anyway. Something certainly makes it work.

And it does. Just ask my friend Doug.

Back on our remote Siberian river, I sit down on a log and watch as Doug clips off his latest exercise in futility and ties on the dearly won GAFF. My shoulder is sore after playing and landing all those fish, so I am content to watch and relax and offer cheap advice. Four dog salmon are enough for the moment, which says something about the limits of the species' appeal. After all, no one ever gets tired of catching big rainbows. Still, there is something about a river full of cooperative, twenty-pound gamefish that is impossible to ignore, even if they can be enjoyed by proxy.

Doug studies the water like an Olympic diver atop a three-meter board and then begins to cast. The fly drifts seductively past the dark, vital mass of fish. Nothing happens. Doug clears his throat. "Technique," I mutter *soto voce* to the sky, well aware that an old friendship may well be on the line.

Doug glares theatrically over his shoulder and casts again. This time the line stops midway through the drift, and when the fish erupts from the water, the sense of relief is almost palpable. It sets its shoulders against the current and makes the reel sing, and by the time Doug works it up into the shallows all is well again.

I moisten my palms in the current and immobilize the fish by gently gripping its tail like a handle. After backing the GAFF out of its jaw, I pause and study the *keta* for a moment. The maroon and green flanks seem reptilian; it's easy to imagine this color scheme on a dinosaur. Then there is the kype, the gnarled jaw, and the ferocious teeth, all as finely exaggerated as the features on a Halloween mask. The fish looks like it wants to kick some ass, but that is pure anthropomorphism. All it wants to do is swim upstream, make more *keta,* and live out its days, which can probably be numbered on the fingers of my hands. Talk about biological clocks ticking.

The fish has places to go and so do we. I ease it back into the stream and watch it swim off, unable to explain why this salmon among all the others made me pause and feel the rhythm of life and death pulsing past us in the current. Finally the fish rejoins the teeming mass and disappears, an individual no longer except within the circuits of my memory. There are lessons to be learned from all of this, but I straighten and turn my back to the river, unable to articulate them.

"Looked like we lost you there for a minute," Doug observes. I shrug. I know Doug understands. He is a thoughtful person and most thoughtful people who spend time next to salmon streams eventually find themselves involved in the pathos of the experience. "Let's go bear hunting," he finally suggests.

When we turn and set off upriver toward camp and our bows and arrows, it feels as if we are racing the *keta* upstream toward the fate that awaits us all.

JASON BORGER

BE PART OF THE BIG PICTURE.

For over 25 years the FFF has rolled-up its sleeves in the fight to conserve and restore wild fish populations around the world.

We have championed international acceptance for "catch & release" as a management tool to ensure quality sportfishing for present and future generations.

And we have introduced countless thousands of all ages to the beauty of our sport.

Be part of the big picture. Help conserve, restore and educate in the name of flyfishing.

Join the FFF. Flyfishing will be better tomorrow!

 FEDERATION OF FLY FISHERS
Conserving – Restoring – Educating Through Fly Fishing
200 Yellowstone Avenue, P.O. Box 1088
West Yellowstone, MT 59758 • (406) 646-9541

(Copy coupon rather than cutting page)